The ETF Trend Following Playbook

The ETF Trend Following Playbook

PROFITING FROM TRENDS IN BULL OR BEAR MARKETS WITH EXCHANGE TRADED FUNDS

TOM LYDON

Vice President, Publisher: Tim Moore
Associate Publisher and Director
  of Marketing: Amy Neidlinger
Executive Editor: Jim Boyd
ditorial Assistant: Myesha Graham
Operations Manager: Gina Kanouse
Senior Marketing Manager: Julie Phifer
Publicity Manager: Laura Czaja
Assistant Marketing Manager: Megan Colvin

Cover Designer: Alan Clements
Managing Editor: Kristy Hart
Project Editor: Anne Goebel
Copy Editor: Krista Hansing Editorial
  Services, Inc.
Proofreader: Apostrophe Editing Services
Indexer: Lisa Stumpf
Compositor: Jake McFarland
Manufacturing Buyer: Dan Uhrig

© 2010 by Pearson Education, Inc.
Publishing as FT Press
Upper Saddle River, New Jersey 07458

This book is sold with the understanding that neither the author nor the publisher is engaged in rendering legal, accounting, or other professional services or advice by publishing this book. Each individual situation is unique. Thus, if legal or financial advice or other expert assistance is required in a specific situation, the services of a competent professional should be sought to ensure that the situation has been evaluated carefully and appropriately. The author and the publisher disclaim any liability, loss, or risk resulting directly or indirectly, from the use or application of any of the contents of this book.

FT Press offers excellent discounts on this book when ordered in quantity for bulk purchases or special sales. For more information, please contact U.S. Corporate and Government Sales, 1-800-382-3419, corpsales@pearsontechgroup.com. For sales outside the U.S., please contact International Sales at international@pearson.com.

Company and product names mentioned herein are the trademarks or registered trademarks of their respective owners.

Printed in the United States of America

Second Printing October 2009

ISBN-10: 0-13-702901-2
ISBN-13: 978-0-13-702901-3

Pearson Education LTD.
Pearson Education Australia PTY, Limited.
Pearson Education Singapore, Pte. Ltd.
Pearson Education North Asia, Ltd.
Pearson Education Canada, Ltd.
Pearson Educación de Mexico, S.A. de C.V.
Pearson Education—Japan
Pearson Education Malaysia, Pte. Ltd.

Library of Congress Cataloging-in-Publication Data

Lydon, Tom, 1960-
  The ETF trend following playbook : profiting from trends in bull or bear markets with exchange traded funds / Tom Lydon.
    p. cm.
  Includes bibliographical references.
  ISBN-13: 978-0-13-702901-3 (hardback : alk. paper)
  ISBN-10: 0-13-702901-2
  1. Exchange traded funds.   2. Stock index futures.   3. Investments.   I. Title.
  HG6043.L928 2010

  332.63'27--dc22

                                                                    2009022712

Thanks to Mom and Dad; my wife, Lisa Ann; our kids, Creagan, Cameron, and Anya; and Lily, our dog, for their love and support

Table of Contents

Acknowledgments

I'd like to thank the numerous people who generously gave us their time and shared their thoughts about ETFs, including the many readers of ETFTrends.com and fellow investment advisors, whose ideas, feedback, and opinions are what made this book possible. I'd especially like to thank the ETF Trends readers who shared their thoughts on investing with us, including William Doherty, Bill Fritz, Hamish Gunn, Bryant Hayward, Roger Hing, Rick Holbrook, and Ted Spickler.

Thank you to all of our ETF industry friends, fellow bloggers, and personal friends, including Larry Connell, Gary Gordon, Bob Grayson, Ted Kennedy, Phil Pegram, Bob Pisani, and Peter Tolk.

Thanks to the team at Jennifer Connelly Public Relations: Jennifer Connelly, Melinda Staab, and Carol Graumann. Thanks also to Darlene March at March Media Relations.

Thanks to Werner Keller, Chip Norton, and Steven Vames for sharing their valuable expertise and knowledge with us to make this a better, more informative book for our readers.

Thank you to John Bishop, who shared his experience and thoughts with us and gave an honest, page-by-page critique of the book.

Thank you to Max Chen, Kevin Grewal, and Tisha Guerrero for sharing their talent for writing and helping make ETF Trends a better web site.

Thanks to all the ETF Trends advertisers who keep the site going and growing.

I'd like to thank Jim Boyd, Anne Goebel, Kristy Hart, and Julie Phifer at FT Press for taking us on once again and guiding us.

Thanks to Virginia Zart and Melody Harris for their day-to-day support and for putting up with me.

A special thank you to Karen Riccio for leading this project. Another special thank you to Heather Hayes for seeing this through to completion with the same care she used in our first book.

Finally, thanks to Mom and Dad and to my wife, Lisa Ann; our kids, Creagan, Cameron, and Anya; and Lily (our dog), for their love and support.

About the Author

Tom Lydon is the proprietor of ETF Trends, a web site with daily news and commentary about the fast-changing trends in the exchange traded fund (ETF) industry. Mr. Lydon is also president of Global Trends Investments, an investment advisory firm specializing in the creation of customized portfolios for high-net-worth individuals. He has been involved in money management for more than 25 years. Mr. Lydon began his career with Fidelity Investments and was a founding member of Charles Schwab's Institutional Advisory Board. He also serves on the board of directors for U.S. Global Investors, Inc.; Security Global Investors/Rydex Investments; and the Pacific Investment Management Co., LLC (PIMCO), Advisory Board for Registered Investment Advisors. Mr. Lydon is a regular contributor to major print, radio, and television media and has been invited to speak to audiences at financial conferences around the world. Mr. Lydon is the author of *iMoney: Profitable Exchange-Traded Fund Strategies for Every Investor.*

Introduction

BUY–AND–HOLD: REST IN PEACE

For decades, the vast majority of us have enjoyed opportunities to improve our personal economic situations. Appreciation in our home, a steady job, growing industry, and continual rises in the stock market are sometimes taken for granted. But the things investors were once able to bank upon are no longer there. Buying and holding stocks can no longer be counted upon as sure things for success.

Our current century hasn't started off so well, and you and millions of others are being forced to rethink your investment strategies to survive. The markets certainly saw their fair share of volatility before now, but this is different. Times have changed.

For much of modern investing history, you and countless other investors have heard that buy-and-hold was the way to go. Experts have assured us that, no matter what happens in the markets, they always trend up over time. If you could just hang on and ride it out, you would be duly rewarded with a handsome retirement fund.

But during the last half of the 2000s, you and millions of others have lived through events rarely seen in history. The nation's largest financial institutions were felled by both a lack of accountability and a lack of transparency. It was an economic crisis for the history books, likely to be dissected and analyzed for years to come.

In the end, if you were among those who held on for dear life, believing that buy-and-hold would prevail, you wound up losing big. Your plans for a comfortable retirement are now dashed. Accountability and transparency seem nonexistent. The net result is that you and others have not only lost big bucks—you have probably also lost faith.

What eventually became known as the United States' "Lost Decade" began well enough when markets hit highs in March 2000. But it wasn't meant to last. For the next few years, a large, unruly bear came in and tore the house down. Technology and the bursting Internet bubble led the big decline, ultimately taking down the NASDAQ Composite (generally referred to as "the NASDAQ" throughout this book) and S&P 500 by 75% and 45%, respectively.

A brief honeymoon lifted the markets from 2003 to 2006, giving investors a reason to believe once again—but along came 2007 and the kickoff of a new bear. This one was the bear of nightmares, some might say. At the end of 2008, the NASDAQ closed down a dismal 41%. The S&P 500 fell 39%—and continued to lose into 2009.

There's always a bogeyman in these markets, right? Savings and loans, dotcoms, oil and gas. The new object of scorn in the markets was real estate—strange and complicated bets, the revelation of a slimy subprime mortgage business, and the ultimate dismantling of some of the world's largest banks and brokerages.

The old way of doing things is worth revisiting, now more than ever. Boom-and-bust cycles are coming with greater frequency and more intensity, eroding the "sure thing" status that buy-and-hold once had. In fact, I'll show you evidence that buy-and-hold hasn't been working anymore and what you can do about it.

I'll give you several examples of market uptrends and downtrends and how to identify them using the 200-day moving average. I'll show you how to apply this strategy to industry-specific markets and sectors in the United States and abroad.

In the end, you will be confident and armed with an easy-to-understand, nonemotional investment strategy that works in any market climate. Up, down, sideways, and no-ways, you'll walk away with the tools you need to put trend following to work, to make money and protect your assets with a disciplined investment strategy.

Now is the time to take a more active role in your portfolio by following the trends using a simple strategy that can help protect you on the downside while having you in the markets for potential long-term uptrends.

What can you gain from all this? You will have peace of mind. You will know how to manage your emotions. You will know that you can make money in any kind of market and avoid those bubbles, booms, and busts that have plagued so many other investors.

What are you waiting for? Let's get started!

chapter 1

Trends Are an Investor's Best Friend

Of all the things you can teach yourself to become a better investor, the best thing is to learn how to identify trends. You probably do it now, to a degree. Perhaps when you heard that oil was nearing $100 a barrel in 2008, you noticed the uptrend. When you heard about bidding wars over houses, you noticed that real estate was trending higher, too. Although you might be familiar with what a bear market or a bull market looks like, to spot trends, you'll have to zoom in a little closer.

Often by the time news of a trend spreads to the point where it's cocktail-party fodder, the bulk of the profits have been made. What you need to do instead is learn to spot trends as early as possible in order to enjoy the longest ride possible.

Figure 1.1 shows the long upswings the market has experienced, followed by equally long corrections. In some cases, these corrections have been devastating. For example, investors who bought in late 2002 would have realized nice gains until about 2007, when the bottom dropped out.

Had you who patiently waited as the S&P 500 climbed and climbed, then hung on as it fell, you would have seen six years go down the tubes.

Believe it or not, you don't have to just sit there. Very few people predicted either of these two bear markets, but investors could have avoided much of the damage to their portfolios simply by following the general market trends.

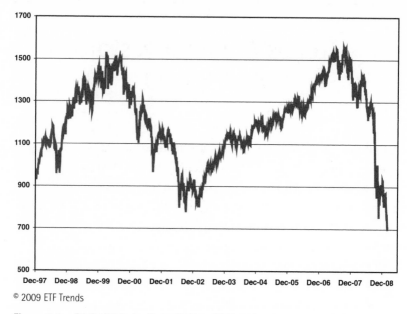

© 2009 ETF Trends

Figure 1.1   *S&P 500 Index from 1997 to 2008*

There is a simple approach that has been used to identify trends for decades. It involves a simple mathematical calculation that identifies general market trends. It's a strategy I've used for my own clients for many years. In Chapter 3, "Spotting Trends," I will show you how it works, what it means, and places you can go for the most current information on trend lines. The concept is simple. Take a look at Figure 1.2. Imagine if you were in the market when the S&P 500 rose above its 200-day moving average, and you were out when it fell below that mark. You could have avoided extended losses simply by being out, and you could have profited by being in at the right times.

But don't stop here. You can apply this trend following strategy anywhere—to any time period, in any market, with any security type. Go ahead and apply the same logic to the devastating technology-driven bear market of 2000–2002 in Figure 1.3.

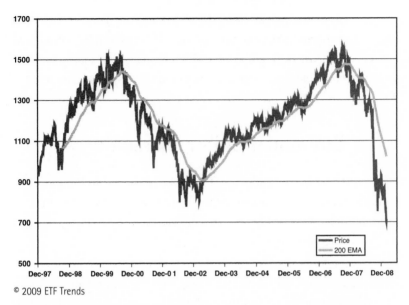

© 2009 ETF Trends

Figure 1.2   S&P 500 Index with 200-day moving average from 1997-2008

© 2009 ETF Trends

Figure 1.3   *NASDAQ Composite with 200-day moving average from 1997-2008*

If you are among the millions who bought technology stocks in the 1990s, only to hold them through one of the most devastating bear markets, you lost as much as 60%–70% in many cases and have still not even come close to recouping that money. But just as damaging as losing money is the loss of time.

Buy-and-Hold's Funeral March

Some of you may be thinking, "What ever happened to the buy-and-hold strategy? It has worked for me for 40 years." Well, that may be true, but take my word for it—and the word of many others: It won't work moving forward.

You might want to be sitting down for this: Buy-and-hold is dead. (And there's no Easter Bunny, either.) Wall Street's mantra is losing steam and support fast and furiously. Investment pioneers Benjamin Graham, Warren Buffett, and Burton Malkiel spewed the virtues of buy-and-hold for years, but the ugly truth is if you are among the investors who have followed this strategy so far this century, you have lost money.

In fact, Buffett reportedly lost more than $16 billion in 2008, enough to make Graham squirm in his grave. While that figure doesn't represent the average investor's losses, it shows just how disastrous buy-and-hold can be.

The bottom line is, buy-and-hold simply hasn't worked. If you're already in retirement or are planning retirement, you might be in a terrible situation. The fact that you've lost money and that there's nothing you felt you could have done about it has had a drastically negative effect on your future plans. You might have considered going back to work part-time, or you might have had to call off retirement for now. It's an ugly scenario for someone to be in, and it's even uglier when you consider that many people could have avoided it altogether.

The country is in the middle of a major influx of baby boomers who are now moving into retirement, but many of them are finding themselves in the uncomfortable position of having to put off what, just five years ago, was a certainty.

For example, let's say that you're a buy-and-hold investor who had planned on retiring in 2009. You're turning 66, you know that you have the money to do it, and you are ready. But then a crash comes. Now you've lost 40% of your portfolio. Suddenly, retirement for you seems as far away as childhood. And when will you have the time to make up the money lost? The closer you are to retirement, the less you can afford to hang on and ride both the ups and downs.

You can find evidence of this by looking at the wheel-spinning the markets have been doing: Had you invested in the S&P 500 in 1997 and held on to it through all the ups and downs until early 2009 (and maybe even later), you would be *below* where you started. All told, that's more than ten years of investing with little to show for it outside of dividends. And what's more, you'd be 12 years older. Those of you who are planning for retirement or who are in retirement can tell the rest of you about the pain.

"It's time to unlearn a common myth about investing," Jim Cramer told viewers on CNBC in late 2008. "The best way to invest is not to buy a bunch of stocks and just sit on them." This doesn't happen often, but I agree wholeheartedly with Cramer. Outside of raging bull markets like the one we experienced in the 1990s, the strategy of buying stocks and holding on to them for eternity no longer works. During bear markets, you stand to lose a whole lot of money, and in sideways markets, your assets will flatline.

But here's the rub: The term *sideways market* is somewhat misleading. There's plenty of market activity, but it's in the form of a sharp downward move, followed by a sharp upward move. Sideways markets can wear on your emotions. They're extremely frustrating and, most important, they burn up a lot of time. Have you ever gotten stuck in the snow or mud? The sensation that your wheels are spinning wildly as you dig a deeper and deeper hole is not unlike the feeling some get in markets that are going nowhere fast.

There are a handful of periods in this century where the market has made no money for ten years or more. For example, an investment in stocks that made up the S&P 500 Index during the periods of 1929–1942 (13 years), 1966–1982 (16 years), and 1997–2009 (12 years) would have amounted to no more than a break-even investment.

From 1997 until 2009, the S&P 500 fell in value an average of 0.4% per year. Through the end of 2008, after two devastating market collapses, the S&P 500 returned 7.1% since 1950 and 7.8% since 1980. In 2000–2008, the S&P's performance was down a dismal 4.7%, including dividends. You don't have to retrace the past decade or more to see the damage this outdated strategy can cause.

Listen: Life is short. All of us only have so much time to save for our golden years. I don't know about you, but I certainly don't have ten years' worth of retirement savings to just up and lose—and then slowly but surely make it up until I'm back where I was before, hoping that there's not another bust before I'm sent back to the starting line again. You and other investors simply cannot afford to suffer the drastic losses we saw in the recent bear markets.

I had never quite heard the strategy of buy-and-hold put this way, but I couldn't agree more with Mike Macdonald, an investment portfolio consultant with Toronto-based Second Opinion Investor Services:

> "Buy-and-hold is a platitude that is outdated. Everything and everybody needs to be monitored regularly because it is often an investor's life savings and future lifestyle that is at risk. Buy-and-hold is like an airplane's autopilot. It works great

when everything is going smoothly. Then birds fly into an airplane's engine and the real value of a live pilot is apparent. Unfortunately for investors, most advisors were on autopilot and there was no heroic landing."

Getting in Touch with Your Emotions

When you buy a security at the right time and ride it to new highs, letting go when it suddenly falls on hard times can be difficult—but if you want to protect your money, you must be prepared to hit the eject button. I have compiled stories in this book from investors who struggle with this very thing; attachment can be a very large hurdle to overcome.

It can be frustrating to sell a position, only to see it turn around and hit new highs just when you sell. I won't lie: You have no guarantee that after you sell a position, it won't turn around and rise higher than it was when you sold it.

That's why it's important to ask yourself why you hold each position in your portfolio, as well as what it would take for you to ultimately sell that position. For example, would you be comfortable if it doubled or if it were a ten-bagger? If you lost 50% in a position, is that the point at which you'd sell? Or if you read news that the company had a fundamental change in its growth strategy—would you sell then?

Stocks and mutual fund components are always fluctuating in value. Management in the underlying companies involved must constantly adjust their strategy based on market and economic conditions. How does this affect the way you view each holding in your portfolio?

Studies have shown that we go through a cycle of investor psychology, as shown in Figure 1.4, which typically ranges between two basic emotions: greed and fear.

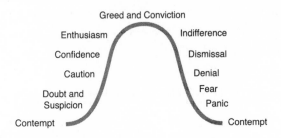

Source: RMB Unit Trusts

Figure 1.4   *The Investor Psychology Cycle*

My trend following discipline eliminates those emotions. Oh, who am I kidding? Let's admit that we're all human. We have powerful feelings and opinions. But when it comes to investing, it's important to quiet them as much as possible. By following a mathematical formula and a disciplined buy-and-sell strategy (and with plenty of practice), you will no longer let these emotions dictate your investment decisions. I'm not saying that you won't experience one or all of them, but they won't prevent you from having the confidence to buy or from pulling the sell trigger.

This brings me to the point of this book. I give you several examples of market uptrends and downtrends, and I show you how to identify them using the 200-day moving average. I also show you how to apply this strategy to industry-specific markets and sectors in the United States and abroad. I give you an easy-to-understand, nonemotional investment strategy that works in any market climate.

Never-Ending Opportunities

"There's always a bull market somewhere" might have become a cliché, but it's certainly true. For example, consider the 2000–2002 bear market—one of the drearier times in stock market history—when average investors lost 50% or more of their retirement assets. However, those who turned to opportunities in utilities, real estate, and precious metals might have avoided loss and instead reaped double-digit returns. Table 1.1 offers a few examples from this dichotic period, to illustrate this point.

Table 1.1 *Areas That Outperformed in Bear Markets*

2000	S&P 500	Home construction	Oil	Utilities
	–10.1%	70.3%	64.3%	53.1%
2001	S&P 500	Home construction	South Korea	Mexico
	–13%	37.2%	44.6%	14%
2002	S&P 500	Commodity Tracking Index	Oil	Energy
	–23.2%	32%	44%	44.3%
2007	S&P 500	Steel	Brazil	Oil
	3.5%	83.1%	72.5%	46.8%
2008	S&P 500	Yen	Gold	Dollar
	–38.5%	22.9%	5.1%	4.2%

Even in the worst of times, when it seems as though everything is crumbling, something good is happening. It's a matter of learning to recognize the signs.

Yes, more evidence of this can be found by looking at the years between 1995 and 2005, when the annual range between the best- and worst-performing sectors was more than 100% in any given year. In 2000, utilities earned 50.5%, while Internet stocks lost 74.5%. In

2004, energy services gained 34.5%, while semiconductors lost 21.6%. The beauty of having a wide range of subsectors at your investment fingertips is that you don't have to rely on the up or down trend of "one" market. Telecommunications isn't doing it for you? Maybe healthcare does. Or perhaps real estate is on another uptrend. When you combine the capability to identify subsectors and trends in the market, it creates more opportunity.

Investor Ted Kennedy, who dodged the 2008 market crash, had this to say: "The 2008 market was the most significant bear market I have ever experienced, and the benefits of a trend following strategy were never more clear." Kennedy notes that: "Protection of capital in significant bear markets has emerged as the most important reason for using this type of strategy."

chapter 2

Risk and Disaster Don't Have to Go Hand-in-Hand

John Bishop, who spent years working as an engineer for Boeing, defines risk in this way:

- A **risk** is the probability of a consequence.
- A **mitigation** reduces the risk's probability or consequence.
- An **issue** is a risk manifested.

Risk is inherent in all corners of the market—from leveraging strategies to Treasury bonds—but a whole bunch of other elements join in to create sheer disaster from it. Most often, the culprit is simply emotions. Perhaps you have rationalized your way out of selling when you should have sold, leading to more losses. Or perhaps you bought in a fit of exuberance without considering whether a position was correct for you, or whether buying entailed more risk than you were willing to take on. Perhaps you were simply too scared to buy. Whatever the reasons, you should know that everyone has been there at one time or another.

The standard argument is that a tactical, active management strategy is risky. And it really is, but only if you don't have a plan or a disciplined strategy. Watch your portfolio quickly dwindle to nothing if you buy and sell on nothing more than a gut feeling. Talk about risk-taking. Another risky move is rationalizing your way out of using your strategy when the time comes.

Risk will never disappear from the markets. It will always remain, and the best you can do as an investor is minimize it. As with all things in life, you can't control the exterior. You can only control your reaction to outside events and how you deal with them, which the trend following strategy sets out to do.

Greed and Fear and Stocks, Oh My!

The largest school of thought blames greed and fear for people making emotionally charged investment decisions. Not to beat a dead horse, but the Internet boom of the late 1990s is a great example. Any advertisement, TV "squawk," or pitch about even start-up Internet-related stocks threw people into such a freakish frenzy that they were dumping conservative S&P 500 index funds making *only* 30% for high-flying triple-digit positions.

Hamish Gunn, an investor in Scotland, fell prey to the comments on message boards and got swept up in the Internet/technology frenzy. "I've slowly learned that it contributed greatly to my problems, in that I believed comments written by people who had an agenda," he says. "I should have done my own research and based my investing on my own ideas." Gunn notes that he followed a high-risk, high-reward strategy. "I never set a stop-loss, thinking all drops would eventually turn."

Sadly, Gunn's story isn't unique. Millions were burned when the technology industry came crashing down on its head. The sad reality is that we'll see this scenario played out over and over for the rest of time. Millions will get soaked in the future when new bubbles float to the surface.

False hopes and a "can't lose" mentality make it nearly impossible to adhere to a strict investment plan, especially amid the "irrational exuberance" of the overall market, as former Federal Reserve Chairman Alan Greenspan put it. At times like these, it's crucial for you to maintain an even keel and stick to a disciplined buy-and-sell strategy.

In fact, greed can compound your woes: Just as the market can become overwhelmed with greed, the same can happen with fear. When investors lose the shirts off their backs, they fear losing their entire wardrobe. Following a bust, typically investors make a mad run for the door, taking money out of equity positions in search of supposedly less risky positions, such as burying cash under a Posturepedic mattress.

Investors are an emotional bunch of people, reacting sharply to both negative and positive news. This isn't good. Overcorrecting can crash your car, and it can crash your portfolio, too.

Running Scared

In 2002, the markets saw the largest amount of outflows in the equity markets since 1988, while a then-record $140 billion flowed into bonds from investors looking for a safety net. Investors threw their plans out the window because they were scared, overrun by a fear of sustaining further losses. Granted, losing a large portion of an equity portfolio's worth is a tough pill to swallow, but even harder to digest is the thought that the more conservative positions have very little chance of ever rebuilding that wealth.

Fear is a tough emotion to deal with and overcome. Investor Ted Spickler suffered through some market whipsaws in the 2008 bear, and he seems to be finding himself more risk averse. "In the current craziness, it's very scary to do anything. My fundamental attitude is scared—to make a decision, to say 'buy' or to say 'sell.'" Fortunately, he has most of his portfolio on the sidelines and has held on to the majority of his retirement money. But not all investors have been so lucky, whether they were too paralyzed to sell or they bought into the buy-and-hold fallacy.

Just as scrapping your investment plan to hop on the latest get-rich-quick investment can tear a large hole in your portfolio, so can getting swept up in the prevailing fear of the overall market by switching to low-risk, low-return investments. It's easy to become swept up, too, when you see how scared others around you are.

Interestingly, the risk factor has been shown not to enter our heads until money has been lost. In fact, you should always consider the downside risk, not just the potential for profit. But we tend to exhibit riskier behaviors in good times, and we batten down the hatches when it's bad.

Just look at the housing bubble the U.S. markets experienced in the 2000s. It might have been risky, but it wasn't unusual to see people plunking down every penny to become "house poor." Banks were lending to anyone and everyone. And why not? Real estate always appreciates. This is a can't-lose move! Right?

Hello? Anyone?

After the bottom in real estate collapsed, you may have been hard pressed to find a consumer looking for a loan, or a bank making one. Bad times = risk aversion.

What Kind of Risk Level Can You Tolerate?

How do you determine your level of risk tolerance? If I asked you what percentage of growth you wanted to pursue each year, you'd need to think about what loss you could stomach before answering me. Higher reward always comes with higher risk. If you want to make 30%, you'd better be able to absorb at least that much of a loss. On the other hand, shooting for a more conservative 12% will keep risk more in check.

This is your comfort level with losing some or all of your original investment; the trade-off is that the potential returns are greater. As risk increases, so does the potential for great reward or great disaster. How comfortable are you knowing that you could lose money? How much of a loss would you be able to stomach? Follow Warren Buffett's two basic rules: "Number 1, don't lose money. Number 2, don't forget rule number 1."

When you've figured out your risk tolerance, you're ready to move forward. I can't tell you what your acceptable level of risk is—that's up to you, regardless of your age. Some experts advise a riskier portfolio when you're younger, becoming gradually more conservative as you approach retirement. But if *you* aren't comfortable with a particular level of risk, that's enough reason for you not to take it on. You know how trainers tell you to stop using the treadmill if you feel faint or dizzy? The same holds true with investing.

Determining your risk tolerance is the most important thing you can do before you invest. Financial institutions have "risk calculators" online to help you determine your comfort level by asking you a series of questions. Answer honestly to get a good result. Enter *investment risk calculator* into the search engine of your choice, and you should see plenty of options to help you.

This is where trend following comes in, too. Although some segments of the market are riskier than others (for example, oil is volatile, whereas a broad fund focused on a stable, developed market won't show wild swings from day to day), a strategy of watching the trends will help you control your overall level of risk and give you a safety net.

Using the 200-day moving average provides sound judgment and rationale for both getting into and getting out of the markets. It gives you an escape hatch, so you don't have to watch in panic as your portfolio hemorrhages. This strategy isn't about trying to call tops or bottoms in the market, or making predictions that never pan out.

Decisions made within the plan are based solely on what is actually happening and nothing else.

Bill Fritz, an investor who lives in the greater St. Louis, Missouri, area, has been using the 200-day moving average strategy since the mid-1980s: "When it's above the 200-day moving average, I'm 100% in. When it's below, I'm 100% out." He compares trend following to a surfer always looking for a good wave. "You hop on the wave, and before it comes crashing on your head, you get off. You may wait awhile for the next wave, or you may jump on another one immediately."

Types of Risk

Not all areas of the market are equally risky. There is also an inverse relationship between risk and reward. High risk equals high reward potential (or equally high disaster potential). Perhaps you're willing to give up some market opportunity for a little more safety. Your returns may not be as nice, but you'll have more security. Or perhaps you want to roll the dice and try for some big returns, and you're even willing to accept the fact that you could lose.

In every scenario, there are trade-offs. It's important to ask yourself what you're willing to take on and really get in touch with, and what events would make you extremely uncomfortable versus what events you can live with.

Aside from market risk, there are many other types as well: Two others to be mindful of are

- **Liquidity risk**—The risk that a security will not be able to be sold because of a lack of liquidity in the market. Liquidity risk is often found in emerging markets or areas of the markets where trading volume is extremely low.
- **Inflation risk**—The possibility that the value of assets will

decrease as inflation reduces the purchasing power of a particular currency.

Staying Grounded

Risk, greed, and fear can certainly play a huge role in your ability to make money. We're all at risk of being swayed by something we read or hear. Many of us feel that our best market indicators are our stomachs.

Being disciplined is key, and the best way to remain that way is to reserve your emotions for Valentine's Day. Don't fall in love with any positions. Just turn and walk away when the numbers dictate that you sell.

Is Time on Your Side?

Along with risk tolerance, you should know your time horizon. This is the expected number of months, years, or decades you will be investing to achieve a particular goal. The longer the time horizon, the more time you have to recover from downturns in the market. On the other hand, if you're saving up for something a few years down the road, you won't likely want to take a big gamble. And if you're relatively close to retirement, don't put most of your money in the stock market and leave it there.

Which category do you feel most resembles your time horizon and risk tolerance?

The Go-Getter (Aggressive)

You're a young 20-something. You've just entered the workforce, perhaps in your chosen field of study, and now you're in it for the long haul. You've got lots of time to prepare for retirement and you don't need the money right now, so you're prepared to stomach a considerable amount of risk if it means being comfortable in 40 years. You want to maximize return and, therefore, be as aggressive as you can possibly be.

The In-Betweener (Somewhat Less Aggressive)

By now, perhaps you've gotten married and maybe even had a few children. You have to start thinking about where your children will go to college. Perhaps you just bought a house, too. You still want growth in your portfolio at this point, but you're slowly easing off the pedals as the years inch along. You're not going to be as aggressive as you were in your early 20s.

The Almost There (Moderately Conservative)

You're pretty close to retirement, and maybe you've got kids headed to college. You might be close to paying off your house, and you're gearing up for some pretty sweet golden years. You need a little bit of income to make up the difference and fill in a few gaps here and there, but you also want to maintain some growth while adding stability to your portfolio, because you're not quite at the finish line yet.

The I'm Outta Here (Conservative)

You're free! You're at the finish line. Retired. *Finito*. Let the fun begin! If you've invested wisely throughout the years, gradually making your portfolio more conservative, you should have a nice amount of money to get you through. You can spoil your grandkids, surprise your spouse with a trip to Europe, or just take it easy and enjoy the simple things. Now your portfolio is aimed at getting some income; growth is no longer the big concern here.

Wherever you are in life, young or old, it's always important to assess your current status and make sure your portfolio reflects all the elements mentioned earlier. Your portfolio should reflect not only where you are in life, but your tolerance for risk.

Taking Too Much Risk? Blame It on DNA or Hormones

A study by Northwestern University researchers says there may be a link between two genes and whether we are aggressive or conservative investors. Sixty-five people (two-thirds women, one-third men) answered 96 questions about how they would use $30 in real money in a computerized investment game. Each participant provided a saliva sample so that researchers could examine their DNA.

The scientists discovered that those with two versions of a particular gene invested 28% less of their money in a risky (but potentially more profitable) fund than did people with other gene combos. Similarly, those with a different version of the gene invested 25% more of their money in the risky fund than those with other variations of that gene.

Scientists are increasingly studying the potential effect of genes and the brain on financial decision making, a field called neuroeconomics. Keep in mind that only about 20% of the difference results from genes, says study coauthor Camelia Kuhnen, an assistant professor of finance at Northwestern's Kellogg School of Management. "I wouldn't want to oversell this as a screening device to find good traders," Kuhnen told *Scientific American.* "Even if I have a gene that predisposes me to taking a lot of financial risk, I could go through a stock market crash that will make me less risk-taking."

Is risk-taking a guy thing, too? Previous research has suggested that high levels of testosterone may cause someone to take on more risk. Men with more of the sex hormone made riskier investments than guys with lower levels, according to a study published in *Evolution and Human Behavior*.

Men with 33% more testosterone than average invested 10% more of their money. The findings are based on saliva samples from 98 male Harvard students taken before they played an investment game with $250 in real money. Even masculine facial features such as prominent jaws and cheek-bones played a role in risk. These students invested 6% more of it than their softer-featured peers.

Interestingly, Anna Dreber, a coauthor of the study, says traders have been shown to make more money on days when their testosterone levels are higher. "Long-term, above-average testosterone levels may perhaps eventually lead to irrational risk-taking, and thus lower profits," Dreber says.

Though the scientists didn't study women, she adds that "women tend to be more risk-averse when it comes to financial gambles. They tend to trade less and that tends to be a better strategy. With more 'average women' trading, maybe the stock market would look different."

What Kind of Investor Are You?

Sometimes it helps to have a specific set of questions to ask yourself before you decide to invest in the markets. Make sure your answers are honest to give yourself a clear picture of who you are and what you can take, and to be sure that you're ready.

- How do you feel about losing money?
- At what point does the thought of losing money make you uncomfortable?
- How much volatility can you handle? Are you willing to ride out sharp swings for potential long-term gains, or would you rather have slow, steady progress?
- Do you have money set aside for the things you need, or are you putting it all in the markets?
- Do you understand what you're about to buy, or are you letting the chips fall where they may?
- How quickly do you expect to see results? Are you patient?
- Are you close to retiring, or have you just graduated college?

chapter 3

Spotting Trends

Buy low and sell high. Boy, that sounds easy, doesn't it? But if you've tried it, you know that it can be next to impossible to accurately do 100% of the time—and it really can't be done without a whole lot of stress.

Wouldn't it be great if instead you could somehow see when a trend might be coming or going? That way, if an uptrend developed, you'd know you had the green light to allocate assets. On the other hand, if a trend turned negative, you could avoid potential serious losses by selling early in the downswing.

Good news! It's possible. You can use moving averages—particularly the 200-day moving average—to monitor trends and make wise investment decisions. I've been using this strategy for years without a crystal ball.

Tools of the Trade

Investors can use a number of investment vehicles to participate in trends: stocks, mutual funds, and exchange traded funds (ETFs). You can find trends using any investible securities you like, although I prefer ETFs.

- **Stocks**—Stocks are shares in publicly held companies. If you buy one share of Google (GOOG) stock, you own a small part of that company. Often investors purchase shares to make a bet not just on a sector but on a specific company within that sector. For this reason, owning single stocks can subject you to more volatility and higher risk (and potentially greater reward). Picking a stock can be very challenging. The fewer stocks you own, the less diversified you are as well.

- **Mutual funds**—Mutual funds are a basket of securities with a manager behind them moving things in and out to achieve a stated objective. When you purchase a share in a mutual fund, you own a part of everything in the fund.

- **Exchange traded funds (ETFs)**—ETFs are similar to mutual funds, in that they are baskets of stocks. But they are generally unmanaged and trade all day on an exchange like a stock. They're most often based on an underlying index, so they tend to be cheaper, on average, than most mutual funds. I go into more detail on ETFs and their many benefits in Chapter 5, "The Nuts and Bolts of ETFs."

Learning to Identify Trends

You may have heard or read about moving averages, or it could be a completely foreign concept to you. Either way, after reading this chapter, you'll be able to explain the 200-day moving average to everyone you know. You'll be able to make trades that help you profit and protect your assets. And you'll be able to impress people at parties.

It helps to understand first what the 200-day moving average is all about before you make it the most-used tool in your toolbox. Used by market technicians and analysts throughout the financial industry, this average is based on a mathematical formula that encompasses a 200-day window and determines the mean (the average) price of a security in that period. As the name suggests, the average moves and changes on a daily basis. The end result after 200 days of data is a smooth, sloping line that defines the overall trend.

Moving averages reflect an accurate and precise snapshot of the markets and can trigger buys or sells. The 200-day moving average can slant in one of three directions: up, down, or sideways. But as with everything in life, I must caution that there are no guarantees.

How can the moving average help you? It helps to give you a picture of a clear uptrend, thanks to its characteristic smooth line. This can be especially helpful when markets are going herky-jerky. In those instances, it can be difficult to see the big picture.

Instead of giving a snapshot of the sharp day-to-day movements or becoming mired in them, the moving average tells you where things are headed overall. If it's sloping downward, you know to steer clear. If it's gradually moving upward, you're seeing some progress. The moving average allows you to see the forest and the trees.

The Rules of the Game

The trend following discipline is so simple that any investor can employ it. The rules are as follows:

1. Buy when a position moves above the 200-day moving average.
2. Sell when a position moves below the 200-day moving average.
3. Leave your emotions at home. If you catch yourself rationalizing your way out of buying or selling when it's appropriate, stop.

Figure 3.1 shows the S&P 500 with its 200-day moving average. You can see when you would be in the market (when the S&P is above the trend line) and when you would be out (when the S&P is below the trend line).

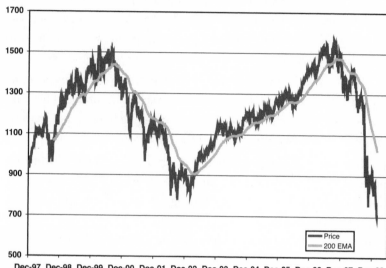

Figure 3.1 *S&P 500 Index with 200-day moving average, 1997-2008*

When a stock or fund moves above or below its 200-day moving average, you can never know whether the trend will be short, moderate, or long-term. But look at it this way: If you're investing on "hunches" or what a friend told you, are you ever really certain?

If a trend turns out to be long or moderate, you're in the money. If it turns out to be a whipsaw—moving above, then below in a short amount of time—having a sell strategy will protect you from any big losses.

Understanding the Moving Average

Moving averages come in two different kinds: simple and exponential. A simple moving average is an arithmetic mean. For example, to calculate a 200-day simple moving average (SMA), you add the closing prices from the last 200 trading days and would divide that figure by 200.

On the other hand, an exponential moving average (EMA) weights the most recent price data most heavily. This type of moving average reacts faster to the most recent price changes than the simple moving average does. The formula for the weighting of the current trading day's value is 2 divided by (200+1). You then add this day's result to the previous calculations, as illustrated in the following sidebar.

EXPONENTIAL MOVING AVERAGE

EMA = (P * α) + (Previous EMA * (1 − α))

P = Current Price

α = Smoothing Factor = $\dfrac{2}{1 + N}$

N = Number of Time Periods

For my own purposes, I use the exponential moving average. Weighting recent price data more heavily attempts to speed up any signals. The disadvantage of doing this, of course, is that this more rapid signal can sometimes be premature and cause a whipsaw.

Exiting Safely and Profitably

"Buying is easy and selling is hard." Isn't that the truth? Even the most seasoned investor struggles to overcome the nagging feeling that if he can just hold on a *little bit longer*, the trend will come back.

Investor and recent retiree Ted Spickler says, "I have been much weaker exiting than entering. It's hard, because I'll be confounded by technicals versus fundamentals. I still have an energy ETF that has just...talk about a massive loss."

Spickler is still holding on to that energy ETF on information about long-term fundamentals, such as that oil will be harder to come by. But logically, Spickler knows, "You've got to get out. Forget the fundamentals. It's hard to say 'Wait a minute. I have to follow these rules.'"

The exit strategy in my plan is this: If a position falls below its 200-day moving average, sell it. As soon as this happens, it's time to let go. It's a rigorous discipline and applies to all asset classes, sectors, and global regions. It's clear-cut, and you know exactly what your risk is.

Although I am a clear proponent of having an exit strategy, it's important to understand that, after you sell, the position can always rebound and go back above its trend line. Oh, I know—it's annoying. But it happens. Forget about it, and learn to keep your eyes ahead. Looking back will only hinder you.

As I've mentioned before, it's also important to appreciate cash as an asset class. When you sell a position after owning it for an extended period of time, or when a whipsaw occurs, you can treat the cash you have as a free agent. This also means that no rule says you must buy back the same, or similar, position that you just sold.

"In my 12 years of moderate investing, money has been made and portfolios have seen their worst," says investor John Bozakis.

The moral, he says? "Take profits and move on."

Sharp market movements and subsequent declines can unsettle many investors. However, using an exit strategy with specific stop-loss points makes the drops less stressful for you, preventing small losses from turning into there-goes-my-house losses.

Avoiding a Bursting Bubble

Bubbles have always formed and will always be created. The only sure way to protect yourself is to have an exit strategy ready.

If a position you're holding—whether commodities or something else—drops below its trend line (200-day moving average), let it go, no questions asked. One way to avoid missing a sell point is to set up e-notifications that a position is about to hit one. Many finance sites offer this, and I cover some of them in the tools section in Chapter 6, "Tools You Can Use."

Investor Larry Connell told me a story about a significant portion of his money that was resting in Boeing (BA) stock. Without a sell point, he clung to the stock for dear life before one day deciding that if it reached a certain price point, he would sell. In January 2005, he finally let it go, at $50 per share.

Wouldn't you know, as soon as he sold, it reversed course. By mid-2007, it had reached more than $100 a share. "At the time, I was hurt," Connell says. But now he's breathing a sigh of relief: In February 2009, Boeing was trading at around $30 per share. "At times, there are problems," Connell admits. "But in the big picture, it works."

Around the time he let Boeing go, he also sold Rockwell Automation (ROK) and Rockwell Collins (COL), both of which have also declined sharply. "If I had held on to those three stocks, look how much I would have lost," he says.

Learning to Live with "the Sell"

Most investors are taught early on to buy a position with the idea that they'll own it for a long period of time. These investors are also taught that, for a sell to occur, something must radically change with the company or the economic environment. Selling under such circumstances implies that there's something better out there for an investor to buy and that there's a better use for this money. But this isn't always so, and breaking free from this thinking will make you a more confident investor.

In the last decade, investors have been more comfortable accepting cash, money market funds, and certificates of deposit (CDs) as an asset class. Just because you've sold something doesn't mean that you have to buy something else today—nothing might be deserving of your money at the moment you sell.

Most people have trouble pulling the trigger when the time comes because it's implied that if you sell, you've somehow failed. This is especially true if you're taking a loss. And if your mindset is that there's something better to buy, and you lack the confidence to buy something else, you won't sell your current position in the first place.

Many investors find that it helps emotionally to explore fundamental reasons why a position either makes sense or no longer does make sense. On the buy side, while you're still following that technical discipline, sometimes finding fundamental reasons that support your decision makes the buy easier. This helps on the sell side, too.

You can argue either side, but doing this can help make you more comfortable with buying or selling when the signals say yes but your fears are telling you no.

Finding the Trends

One aspect of trend following is the ability to locate trends, which might seem obvious. And this is easy in good markets. But in late 2008, as the market went into a free-fall, were you thinking about what was trending up? Probably not. Most investors in this situation tend to think that everything's bad. I assure you, this is generally not the case.

Consider some examples of sectors that ran contrary to the broad market, and think about how each relates to its 200-day moving average.

Up, Down, and Flat as a Pancake

A stock's price can be doing only one of three things: trending up, trending down, or trading in a range. An uptrend is established when a stock undergoes a series of higher highs and higher lows. In a downtrend, it forms a series of lower lows and lower highs. A trading range occurs when a stock cannot establish an uptrend or a downtrend. If a position is in a trading range, an uptrend starts when the upper boundary of the range is broken. A downtrend begins when the lower boundary is broken.

No matter what causes the market to travel sideways, it underscores the inherent danger of the buy-and-hold strategy, especially if you're dealing with unmanaged "index" mutual funds. No one is moving things in or out for you, looking for bright spots and exiting the duds, so you could potentially wind up riding something down for an extended period of time.

Sure, the markets will likely rebound eventually, but that will be of little consolation to investors who need their money soon for retirement or who may have bailed out of the markets at or near the bottom. How long will it take to get them back to where they were? Too long, in many cases.

It's even harder for S&P 500 index investors who relied on this large-cap benchmark to grow their retirement savings. In the Lost Decade, an investor who bought an S&P 500 fund in 1997 was sitting below where he started by 2009. I don't know about you, but I hate wasting time.

To help make my argument, I approached my good friend Werner Keller. Keller is president of Keller Partners LLC, a research firm serving institutional investors. His firm develops mathematical models that analyze the trends of the securities market. In the following sidebar, Keller explains how a trend following strategy versus a buy-and-hold strategy works over an extended period of time.

MARKET TREND IDENTIFICATION WITH LONG-TERM MOVING AVERAGES

Day-to-day stock market movements certainly appear random and impossible to predict. Yet when we step back, the markets of the world do appear to move in large, long-term swings. Investors must position themselves on the right side of these swings, because they play a huge role in long-term success.

Long-term moving averages are, in effect, smoothing filters that tend to screen out the daily noise but capture much of the critical underlying market trend. At the request of our colleagues at ETF Trends, our firm recently examined the long-term performance of the 200-day exponential moving average.

We investigated this question: "How much better off could we have been if we had switched an S&P 500 index portfolio to cash every time that the index value dipped below its 200-day exponential average (EMA), and then reinvested it every time the index crossed back up through this average?"

The answer turned out to be, "Much better off." We retrieved data for the Standard & Poor's 500 Composite back to early 1930, and decided to split the study into two periods of approximately 40 years each: 1930–1970 and 1970–2008. The charts of the index versus the moving average (Figures 3.2 and 3.3) clearly suggest that the 200-day EMA tends to keep the investor on the right side of the major trend *most* of the time (not all the time, but *most* of the time).

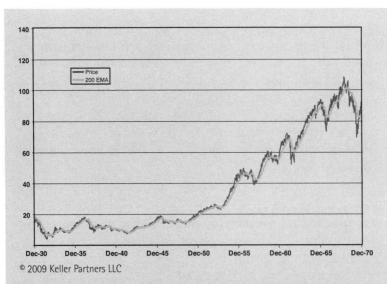

© 2009 Keller Partners LLC

Figure 3.2 *S&P 500 versus 200-day exponential moving average, 1930–1970*

© 2009 Keller Partners LLC

Figure 3.3 *S&P 500 versus 200-day exponential moving average, 1970–2008*

The next two charts (Figures 3.4 and 3.5) show the progression of the portfolio's equity versus buy-and-hold for each period. We assumed that, when the traded portfolio was in cash, it would have earned interest at the rate of 2.0% annually, a conservative assumption that we feel allows room for a management fee, as well as for the occasional transaction costs on the exchange transactions. The improved performance was measured in two critical dimensions: annual return and portfolio drawdown.

For both of the 40-year periods, the moving average portfolios achieved a *measurably higher annual return.* Perhaps even more significant, the path to that return was much more civilized, in that interim losses were much more subdued. The investor was subjected to *dramatically less portfolio drawdown* in both periods. Less drawdown means greater staying power.

—Werner E. Keller, CFA
www.kellerpartners.com

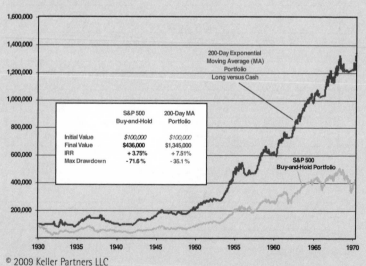

© 2009 Keller Partners LLC

Figure 3.4 *Buy-and-hold S&P 500 versus long/cash 200-day EMA, 1930–1970*

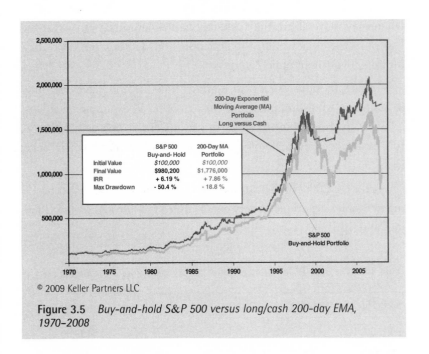

© 2009 Keller Partners LLC

Figure 3.5 *Buy-and-hold S&P 500 versus long/cash 200-day EMA, 1970–2008*

Timing Is Everything

The volatile jerks during a sideways market often make investors feel like Jekyll and Hyde. Market rallies give them cause for excitement, and the sharp downturn that follows sets them into deep depression.

Don't fall for these sudden movements. People who can't stand the fluctuations often get out of the market and sit on the sidelines, with no plan on how to get back in when the market settles into a trend.

Depressed markets will provide great buying opportunities at one point. After all, low sellers reward low buyers. Some of the best buying opportunities follow bear markets. Eventually, investor confidence and trends turn positive, and you must have the discipline to buy when they move above their 200-day moving averages. If you let the fear of losing money enter the equation, you stand to lose once-in-a-lifetime investment opportunities.

In fact, the four worst bear markets since 1922 all have one thing in common: After dropping very close to 50%, all experienced at least a 52% rally, triggering uptrends in various areas such as healthcare, real estate, utilities, technology, natural resources, and financial services.

After the 2000-2002 bear market, check out the types of post-bear market rallies experienced between March 11, 2003, and May 5, 2006, in Table 3.1.

Table 3.1   *The Best-Performing Sectors After the 2000-2002 Bear Market*

S&P 1500 Sector Index*	Return %
Energy	158.00
Materials	118.15
Industrials	105.75
Utilities	95.68
Financials	83.86
S&P Composite 1500 Index	79.04
Consumer Discretionary	73.89
Information Technology	68.39
Telecommunication Services	64.17
Consumer Staples	44.01
Healthcare	31.64

Source: FactSet Research Systems Inc.

*The S&P 1500 Index is an index of U.S. stocks, which includes all the stocks in the S&P 500, S&P 400, and S&P 600.

In down markets, the areas that are beat up vary. Sometimes one or two areas drag the markets down; other times, it's every area. For example, in 2008, every single sector in the S&P 500 took a loss. Financials were the worst, losing 55.3%. Materials lost 45.7%, and information technology declined 43.1%.

Remember, just as we've talked about the emotional part of selling, there's an equally important emotional part of buying. Usually the market turns well ahead of investors' comfort levels, but you must let the numbers tell the story.

The point with a trend following strategy is that the probability of success is higher than it is with other strategies, such as "throw it up and see what sticks."

Protecting your portfolio in down markets and having an exit strategy is important, but the real joy in investing is having the discipline to take advantages of new uptrends that develop.

chapter 4

Why Trend Following Can't Be Beat

The easiest way to explain trend following is to explain what it's not. It's not buying at the bottom, and it's not selling at the top. If you're following trends, you won't be able to do that.

Trend following is a nonemotional, mathematical discipline that's simple for any investor to follow. If you follow it as you should, you'll get the lion's share of any long-term uptrend—and you'll also avoid the lion's share of a long-term downtrend.

Keep in mind that, over time, the stock market and individual securities follow general identifiable trends. The idea is that you want to be more fully invested in stocks when the market is above its long-term trend line (200-day moving average). Similarly, you want to be safely positioned when the market is trending downward.

Figure 4.1 shows the S&P 500 with its 200-day moving average. You can see the periods in which we would have been in (above the 200-day) and when we would have been out (below the 200-day). If you had bought the S&P 500 in the mid-1990s, you would have enjoyed one of the best uptrends in decades.

In this figure, you can see it all: buy signals, sell signals, and whipsaws. Buy signals occur when the S&P crosses above its 200-day moving average; sell signals occur when it drops below. And then we have the whipsaws.

Several times in Figure 4.1, the market peeked above its moving average; if you were following the plan, you would have bought at this time. Eventually, however, you would have sold and exited with a small loss. Whipsaws are never fun, but they're a small price to pay:

You never know when the next buy signal is the beginning of the next long-term uptrend. The key, then, is knowing when to be in and when to be out. Figure 4.2 illustrates the buy-and-sell points you would use with a trend following plan.

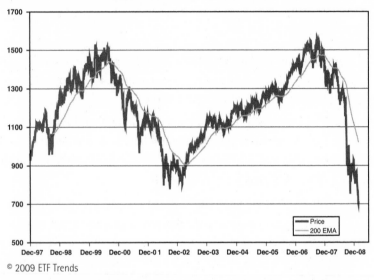

© 2009 ETF Trends

Figure 4.1 *S&P 500 Index with 200-day moving average, 1997–2008*

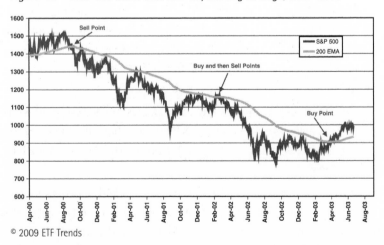

© 2009 ETF Trends

Figure 4.2 *S&P 500 Index with 200-day moving average, 2000–2003*

HOT STOCKS CAN LEAVE NASTY BURNS

When a sector is hot, it's usually because investors have already made big gains. People are talking about it—they're getting in and telling you to join them. It's hard to fight the enthusiasm. But you should resist the temptation to jump on the bandwagon. If a stock gets too hot, mania often surrounds the potential growing bubble. When manias happen, investors lose their heads completely, paying astronomical prices for inflated value.

Investor Hamish Gunn burned himself in the tech bubble of the late 1990s. He notes that he shouldn't have just gone along with what message board participants were saying. Admittedly, he got caught up in the frenzy. Gunn is not alone, though. This scenario happens time and time again throughout history. For example, sometimes technology (such as the Internet) really does change the world. However, our inflated sense of the event led to a market crash.

The same holds true for real estate in the 2000s, when prices doubled and tripled in certain areas of the United States. When someone is telling you that you "can't lose," I suggest that you picture the *Titanic* and remember how well that ended—and it was supposedly "unsinkable!" Everything is sinkable.

Still, if you do get caught up in the mania, don't be too hard on yourself. Investors have been doing it for centuries. Check out these past manias to see for yourself:

The Tulip Mania, Holland, 1634–1637

During the Dutch Golden Age, contract prices for bulbs of the recently introduced tulip reached phenomenally high levels, then suddenly collapsed. For 36 months, prices steadily increased by 5,900% before falling 93%. This is generally considered the first speculative bubble.

The South Sea Bubble, Britain, 1719–1720

The South Sea Company was founded in 1711. It was granted a monopoly to trade in Spain's South American colonies as part of a treaty; in turn, it assumed the national debt that England incurred during the war. Speculation about the South Sea Company's stock led to a bubble for a period of eight months, during which the price increased 1,000% before falling 84%.

As you can see, if you get swept up in a wave of enthusiasm, you can feel somewhat assured that our ancestors have been doing it for hundreds of years.

Never Look Back

Why have an exit strategy? That's simple. Having an escape hatch helps protect any gains you made and also protects your principal. But this works only if you're disciplined in selling when you should. And if you do this, you won't experience those huge long-term declines in the markets that many buy-and-hold investors have in the past.

If you miss getting in a hot sector early, don't beat yourself up over lost opportunity. The trend following plan is all about moving forward and looking for the uptrends; it's not about self-flagellation. Investor Bill Fritz even notes that when you get on that "wave," you're usually not the first one on. It's important to be okay with that. Sure enough, other people eventually join you on the wave. And then you don't hang on until it crashes on your head—you exit and find your new wave.

The market has always experienced, and always will experience, bubbles. The only way to protect yourself is to have a point at which you let go. Sharp market movements and subsequent declines can unsettle many investors. However, having an exit strategy and specific stop-loss points makes the drops less stressful for you by preventing small losses from turning into there-goes-my-house losses.

What Happens After You Sell?

Now that you've had the discipline to follow your strategy, what next?

Try this:

- Treat the newly available cash as "free agent" funds. Just because you sold a position doesn't mean you're obligated to buy it back when it rebounds.
- Look for a position that is above or rising above its trend line. As soon as it crosses, you can consider it a "buy" signal.
- Look for a position with positive, relative strength that is not yet above its trend line, and monitor it so you're ready when it does go above. When markets rebound off a low, those with the greatest momentum usually enjoy sustained uptrends.

What if the position rebounds after you sell it? Don't cry over spilled milk. As you can see, you'll have many other opportunities.

Conquer Volatility, Don't Let It Conquer You

With volatility in the markets over the past couple years, we have seen major price swings in just about every sector. Don't worry about daily price movements, though; having an investment plan is the priority. When you have discipline in place, it can help guide you through these volatile times.

If you've got nervous hands as your positions swing up one day and down the next, the best thing to do is just sit on them. Removing emotion from your investing is one of the smartest things you can do—these days, especially when all the ups and downs can make you feel sick.

Investor Robert Eustace notes that he's been a proponent of trend following for some time. "I was convinced that the trend following approach with stop-loss orders and trailing stop-loss orders was the approach for me even before the recent bear market started." But that doesn't mean he's immune from the feelings that plague all investors. "I now struggle to resist the temptation to buy in before there is a clear trend up," he says

Do You Have Any Better Ideas?

If following trends by using a mathematical formula and sticking to a disciplined sell strategy doesn't appeal to you, what other choices do you have?

You could try to time the market, which involves predicting the best time to buy and sell, trying to buy at the lowest low and sell at the highest high. Studies have shown that if an investor had successfully timed the market since 1950 until today and avoided the

20 worst-performing months for the period, he would outperform an invested-at-all-times strategy by 4.65% annually.

But exactly how simple is it to successfully time the market? I think we'd see a lot more billionaires than we do these days if it were a cinch. Please don't confuse trend following with market timing. They're as different as day and night, and could mean the difference between being wealthy and being poor. Market timing is guessing; trend following is a mathematical strategy. Market timing has quite a few potholes, and it's a strategy that is pretty much impossible to pull off consistently over the long term.

Then there's buy-and-hold.

Buy-and-Hold: Does It Work Like It Should?

If you're this kind of investor, you're doing exactly as the name implies: buying and holding through all the ups and downs. This strategy has been showing more and more cracks in recent years, though. Are you really getting all that you can out of this strategy? Just ask the buy-and-holders of the technology boom and bust. Those who hung on for the entire stomach-churning ride lost trillions hoping their positions would one day rebound.

The crux of the buy-and-hold argument is the efficient market hypothesis, which states that if every security is fairly valued at all times, there's no point in trading. Different investors take this argument to different degrees. Some believe that one should *never* sell. Others believe in the buy-and-hold strategy on cost-based grounds, that it's simply cheaper because the fees incurred on all transactions erode earnings over time.

Not only has the S&P 500 gone nowhere for the last ten-plus years, but Barry Ritholtz at The Big Picture blog pointed out something that might make investors sit up and take notice. If you look at the S&P 500 over the last 109 years, investors will find a number of 20-year periods in which returns were less than 2–3%. If you take into account inflation, some 20- and 30-year periods showed returns that were actually negative.

Now we're beginning to understand why buy-and-hold is often known by the pejorative "buy-and-hope." In some periods, the S&P 500 did exceptionally well, of course: From 1949 until 2000, the index gave a total annual return of 13.1%. But this tells us nothing about the future. John Maynard Keynes, of the well-known Keynesian approach, put it this way: "We simply do not know."

Analyst Peter Bernstein wrote an essay in *The Financial Times* about the death of the buy-and-hold philosophy, in which he said, "How certain can we be that trends are destiny? Trends bend. Trends break. ...There is no predestined rate of return. There is only an expected return that may not be realized." In short, Bernstein is saying that if you're buying and holding, you're really just guessing. There are no guarantees. And history has shown more often than not that investors are left disappointed when they have lofty expectations that go unmet.

Where That Leaves Us

Monitoring trends with the 200-day moving average is the best option in the investment universe. In the next chapter, I talk about my tools of choice, ETFs, and explain why I dropped mutual funds like a hot potato.

By buying this book and reading this far, you've shown that you're obviously committed to playing a greater role in the success of your portfolio. Let's talk about the tools you need to put this plan into serious action.

RESOLUTIONS FOR ALL TIME

Momentum can certainly turn on a dime. Just look at the healthcare sector in 1991 as an example. It was up 50% for that year, but the following year, it was down 19%. But that's the way of the trend—it works, it hums along, it's doing fantastically, until one day it no longer is.

Whatever trend you're following, be sure to take a disciplined approach and follow through with your strategy.

- Resolve to stick to your discipline. It's very difficult to not get emotional, whether that's happiness or sadness. Remove both and focus on finding new waves to jump onto.

- Resolve to pay attention to the news. Political upheaval, major weather events, and leadership changes can indirectly affect your holdings. Don't just isolate yourself to the business section.

- Resolve to pay attention to your investments. Are you coming up on a major life change, such as having children or entering the home stretch before retirement? Look at your portfolio as your life moves into different stages, or if your needs change, and make sure it's still working for you.

- Resolve not to invest in something simply because it's "hot." That's the best way to get burned. Invest because it fits your needs, your interests, and your portfolio.

chapter 5

The Nuts and Bolts of ETFs

As a $9 trillion industry, it's really not fair to say that mutual funds are dead or even dying. But ETFs are giving them a serious challenge for market share, and the events of 2008 could well be the tipping point.

Mutual funds are by far the most popular investment vehicle for the average American. Ask the average Joe who doesn't even invest if he knows what a mutual fund is—of course he does.

It's no wonder then, that investors are increasingly turning to a relatively new alternative: the exchange traded funds (ETFs). They're hardly a household name, but if you hold them up side by side to any mutual fund, their advantages are undeniable. They've got investors of all types, styles, and strategies, very excited.

Investor Bill Fritz uses them to protect his portfolio now that he's retired: "They can trade at anytime during the day."

The trend toward ETFs and the way they're used is leading to a reversal of all the traditionally held notions about investing: buy-and-hold; use mutual funds; don't touch your portfolio until you retire; be risky when you're young and more conservative when you're older. ETFs have a role in changing that thinking.

It's been quietly building for awhile, but I'm seeing a gradual shift away from mutual funds and toward ETFs as the investment of choice for a few reasons:

- **Mutual funds are inherently opaque**—Something many investors accepted until they recently saw their savings seriously damaged in the market crash of 2008, as a more recent example. Mutual funds only have to report their holdings every 90 days. For today's investor, that's often not enough.

- **High fees**—The average expense ratio for a mutual fund is 1.57%. The average expense ratio of an ETF is 0.41%.

- **Capital gains taxes**—Mutual funds have to sell their holdings in order to meet redemptions, which can lead to capital gains taxes whether you sold or not.

- **Poor performance**—Eight out of 10 actively managed mutual funds have underperformed their benchmarks.

- **The Internet**—Let's face it: The Internet has made a lot of things possible. You can find low fares for travel without having to use an agent. You can find coupons. And you can use it to do your own investing research. Thanks to sites like Yahoo! Finance, you can put together your own portfolios and see what's moving and what isn't. Why do you need a fund manager anymore?

Why ETFs Are a Better Solution

ETFs are the brash new kid on the block, offering innovation and a stream of fresh ideas. They're turning a decades-old formula on its head, offering greater flexibility, more opportunities for diversification, and the chance for investors to get in on exciting markets previously closed to them.

Here's what they are and what they do better than mutual funds or individual stocks:

- **Served up in a basket**—Similar to mutual funds, ETFs can pool various securities—stocks, bonds, commodities, currencies—into one package. Typically, these funds have underlying indexes that they track. For example, the S&P 500 Index represents the 500 largest stocks by market value.

The S&P 500 ETF (SPY) is sold as an individual security and listed on an exchange. Investors get exposure to all 500 stocks, but in a far more simple and cost-effective way. After all, do you really want to go out and buy shares for 500 companies? Another important point is that when you're dealing with an index, you have transparency. This means you can *see* what you've invested in. You know what stocks are in your portfolio. For those who got burned in the mutual fund scandals of the early 2000s, the many years of history, trust, and built-in transparency behind indexes is welcome. Indexes don't involve manager risk.

- **Easy trading**—ETFs trade just like stocks. You can buy and sell them through brokers and they are traded throughout the day. Their prices constantly reflect changes in market prices. They're different from mutual funds, in which investors buy shares in a pool of securities, because mutual funds are not listed on exchanges. You can buy ETFs the same way you would a stock, using techniques such as shorting (selling in anticipation of a price drop), using limit-buys, and issuing stop-loss orders. You can't do that with mutual funds.

- **You know what you're buying**—ETF providers publish their holdings every day and note any changes. Most funds that represent an index rarely change at all. You know what you own at all times—what you see is what you get. That's not possible with a mutual fund, which only has to publish quarterly statements and won't fully disclose their trading expenses. As such, ETFs are not subject to the kind of trading abuses that have ravaged mutual funds in the last decade. ETFs are continuously repriced throughout the trading day, so late trading isn't possible. In comparison, the net asset value (NAV) of traditional mutual funds is always a trading day's closing price.

- **Very low cost**—Because holdings in index ETFs are rarely sold, management fees are low. Although you'll pay a brokerage commission to buy or sell them (I recommend working with a deep-discount broker), expenses are minimal in ETFs because they are efficient. Fees gobble your returns, so keeping them as low as possible is to your—and your retirement's—advantage. You're not paying a manager to actively work in the fund, either.

- **Tax friendly**—If a mutual fund has a good year, you'll often pay for it in taxable gains outside of a tax-deferred account. Even in a terrible year, don't be shocked by capital gains distributions from sold holdings. This is because even though a mutual fund has had an overall loss, it will have sold some holdings at a profit. These profits are then distributed as capital gains to all shareholders. Not so in most ETFs, which are largely insulated from the need to sell holdings for shareholder redemptions. Most index ETFs have static portfolios that are passively managed, so they generate gains only if a security needs to be sold because the index keepers have changed the index. So most ETFs don't generate capital gains from buying and selling components; you pay tax only on profits from selling your ETF shares, so you can also control the timing of taxable outcomes. Capital gains distributions can and do happen, though—just not as frequently.

- **Diversification and risk reduction**—Because ETFs are broad baskets of securities, they can represent entire markets. Want to buy a fund representing all listed domestic or foreign stocks? How about sampling most large overseas stocks? Or U.S. bonds? ETFs can do that and more. Exposure to more securities lowers your portfolio risk. You need never buy another single stock again. Why gamble far too much money on what you think will be the next Google when you can buy an entire technology fund full of potential winners from all over the world?

A Fast-Growing Industry

ETFs are flourishing in their popularity. I've been using them to protect my clients' assets for many years now, and it's exciting to be a part of one of the best investment tools to come along in history.

During the 2008 market collapse, ETFs continued to experience net inflows, even as mutual funds hemorrhaged assets. I believe this says more about their benefits than anything else. In a time when investor trust was battered and lost, ETFs emerged with shining colors as the go-to tool for investors looking to know what they own, and at a low cost.

As of February 2009, there were 756 ETFs with $460 billion in assets. That's a dip down from a year earlier: In February 2008, ETFs held $572 billion in assets, but in challenged and depressed markets, that's to be expected.

The breadth of asset classes and sectors that ETFs cover could have had something to do with sustaining investors' interest in them. If real estate is crumbling, for example, investors can seek out other areas, such as fixed income or gold funds, if they're trending up.

In normal markets, ETFs will grab more than their fair share of the assets. The events of 2008 might have hurt everyone in the short term and put a small dent in the ETF industry's total assets, but in the long term, those events will be a key factor in the decisions investors make going forward.

Barclays remains optimistic about the future of the ETF industry. It forecasts that ETF assets under management will exceed $1 trillion in 2009 and $2 trillion in 2011. Financial Research Corp. agrees, predicting that, by 2012, ETFs will represent 6.8% of the retail investment marketplace's total assets.

Although 6.8% might still seem fairly small in comparison to the longtime majority figure for mutual funds, some realities of the asset management industry dictate that ETF gains against mutual funds will continue to be gradual. After all, mutual funds have been around for many decades, and despite all their pitfalls, they still have name recognition and familiarity that ETFs simply don't have yet.

ETFs are fast becoming the investment vehicle of choice for financial advisors. A 2008 Investment News survey showed that 75.6% of advisors are recommending ETFs, and 61.9% are doing so more than they did a year ago. In what could be a harbinger of the long-term relationship between mutual funds and ETFs, 62.8% of advisors have said that ETFs are a complement to mutual funds rather than a threat.

Evaluating ETFs

What happens when you see multiple sectors, regions, or asset classes, or multiple ETFs in an uptrend, and you want a part of the action? How do you choose just one ETF to buy?

As long as you are focused on how much risk you can take, you can ignore the stock market, mutual funds, and stockbroker and Wall Street recommendations. Pick an ETF that is broadly diversified, offers low costs, has crossed its long-term trend line and gives you a break on taxes. How do you gauge the best fund for you?

Consider these guidelines for evaluating different ETFs:

- **How much does it cost?** This answer is found in the fund's *expense ratio,* a percentage of how much a fund manager deducts from your assets annually. Also consider brokerage commissions to buy and sell shares. Consider these industry average expense ratios compiled by Morningstar (www.morningstar.com), the financial information company:

U.S. Fixed-Income ETFs: 0.29%

U.S. Stock ETFs: 0.41%

International Stock ETFs: 0.52%

- **What's in the portfolio?** The fund company will give you a complete list of securities, the rate of *turnover* (what percentage of the portfolio is sold off during a year), and the sectors represented by the portfolio. A portfolio with 50 stocks or less will be more volatile than one with 500 holdings, so keep that in mind when gauging risk. Look for sector weightings, style (growth or value), and composition (percentage of stocks, bonds, cash, and so on). Also look at the top holdings and their weight. A fund with its top three holdings weighted at 50% of the fund might be more volatile than a fund that has the heaviest weighting of a stock capped at 5%.

- **What's the risk level?** Some segments of the market are far more volatile than others. Oil is known for big swings, but something like Treasury bonds will be calmer and steadier. Leveraged ETFs can amplify volatility. How risky do you want to be? Do you want to buy and sell more frequently if you think you can achieve higher returns? You can use the trend following strategy as a measure of protection, but be sure you understand the nature of the fund you're looking at as well.

- **What is the trading volume and asset size?** How actively traded is the fund on the market? How many assets are in it? If both levels are high, you can be sure that it's a liquid security. If those figures are low, you might have a hard time selling it when it comes time to do so. Most individual investors won't be dealing in large volumes, though, so this is a more important point of consideration if you're planning to deal in volume.

- **What is the tax liability?** Few stock ETFs have any tax liability (the amount of capital gains and other taxes generated), but some do. The fund company can give you a breakdown of any taxable distributions. Keep in mind that fixed-income, commodity, and precious-metals ETFs have different tax treatments than stock funds. Of course, if you're concerned about taxable gains, keep in mind that ETFs work within tax-deferred accounts such as individual retirement accounts.

- **What's in *your* portfolio?** What are you already holding? If you've got an oil fund, do you really want to invest in a country such as Russia, which is heavy in energy-related stocks? Even the riskiest risk-taker wants some diversification, to avoid going down with the ship.

Employing ETFs

ETFs got their start in the United States by tracking some of the largest stock indexes, particularly the S&P 500, the Dow, and the NASDAQ. Indexes can give you diversified ownership in entire markets in one package, including products that are difficult to invest in outside of futures exchanges.

ETFs now include everything from the smallest public companies to currencies, and give you access to investments that were challenging to invest in before. They can be solid, long-term investment vehicles—if you stick to a trend following strategy.

SUMMARY OF ETF COMPANIES

The ETF industry is changing constantly. There are hundreds of funds in registration, many from new providers. Here is a list of some of the largest providers* in the United States:

- **iShares** (www.ishares.com)—iShares is the world's largest ETF provider and has nearly 200 ETFs listed in the United States alone. They cover single countries, sectors, commodities, and fixed-income.

- **State Street Global Advisors (SPDRs)** (www.ssgafunds.com and www.spdrs.com)—Perhaps the most well-known funds in this family are the SPDR Gold Trust (GLD), which holds gold bullion, and the SPDR (SPY), which tracks the S&P 500 and is one of the most actively traded ETFs in existence. State Street is also known for their line of S&P 500 sector funds, which focus on financials, healthcare, and more.

- **Vanguard** (www.vanguard.com)—Well-known for their diverse selection of traditional mutual funds, Vanguard also offers a well-rounded set of ETFs ranging from market segments to industry sectors. There are also a few international ETFs that primarily cover whole continents.

- **ProShares** (www.proshares.com)—ProShares offers a line of short and double-short ETFs that have proved to be very popular with investors looking to hedge their positions. They also have a line of ETFs that allow market players to maximize their positions by going double long.

*Providers are listed in order of total assets in the United States.

- **PowerShares** (www.invescopowershares.com)–
  PowerShares offers more than 100 different ETFs. Many
  of the PowerShares ETFs use "dynamic indexing" in
  order to constantly search out the best performing
  stocks within each index.

- **Market Vectors** (www.vaneck.com)–Market Vectors has
  about 15 ETFs that cover a range of industries, from
  nuclear energy to solar energy to coal mining to steel.

- **Direxion** (www.direxionshares.com)–Direxion has an innovative line of triple-leveraged ETFs that allow investors to
  go three times long or short the market. These funds
  cover sectors, fixed-income, and asset classes.

- **WisdomTree** (www.wisdomtree.com)–Wisdom Tree has
  launched a family of ETFs whose underlying stocks are
  weighted based on the amount of dividends they pay,
  as opposed to their total market cap.

- **Security Global Investors/Rydex Investments*** (www.
  rydex.com)–They have a suite of currency ETFs known
  as CurrencyShares, which track the price of various foreign currencies versus the U.S. dollar. They also have
  ETFs focused on broad-based market segments, as well
  as ETFs using equal-weighting strategies.

- **Claymore** (www.claymore.com)–Claymore aims to capture unique areas of the market presently not covered
  by other fund families. Offerings include market segment, market style, specialty sectors, and fixed-income.

- **First Trust** (www.ftportfolios.com)–First Trust has a
  range of global, sector, size/style, and specialty funds,
  which focus on such things as water, green energy, and
  initial public offerings (IPOs).

*Full disclosure: Tom Lydon is a board member of Security Global Investors/Rydex
Investments.

- **Fidelity** (www.fidelity.com)—Fidelity is one of the best-known mutual fund providers, but they do have one ETF, the aptly named ONEQ. Many are looking to this company to get on board with ETFs 100%.

- **RevenueShares** (www.revenuesharesetfs.com)—RevenueShares has a small line of ETFs that seek to hold the same stocks as well-known benchmarks. The twist is that the components are weighted by revenue, not market cap.

- **IndexIQ** (www.indexiq.com)—As of April 2009, IndexIQ has one ETF that uses a hedge fund replication strategy. The provider will soon have a suite of hedge fund replication ETFs.

- **Grail Advisors** (www.grailpartners.com)—They were first on the scene with a qualitative active ETF, which is managed by three veteran mutual fund and institutional subadvisors.

- **Global X** (www.globalxfunds.com)—As of April 2009, Global X has one ETF that targets the volatile market of Colombia. They have other ETFs in registration focused on Egypt, Peru, Argentina, and more.

There are also a number of new ETF provider with funds in registration, including

- **Charles Schwab**—www.schwab.com
- **ETF Securities**—www.etfsecurities.com
- **Pimco**—www.pimco.com

chapter 6

Tools You Can Use

To properly identify changing market trends, you must equip yourself with the necessary tools to do so. Fortunately, the Internet has made this task easier than ever.

News

Sometimes market trends can develop quickly, so it's important to keep your finger on the pulse of what's happening. Television is always a good up-to-the-minute source, and it can be entertaining. But I suggest a few financial web sites instead to capture the major stories of the day.

Among the best general news sites are these:

- **Yahoo! Finance**—www.finance.yahoo.com
- **Smart Money**—www.smartmoney.com
- **Market Watch**—www.marketwatch.com

Web sites such as these can keep you on top of ongoing developments with specific sectors, companies, countries, and so on. They're updated frequently throughout the day as conditions shift. You won't miss a thing. On several of these and other sites, you can set up price alerts so that you won't forget to check your holdings or miss a key sell signal. You can also set up "buy" alerts.

Among the best ETF-specific web sites are these:

- **ETF Trends**—www.etftrends.com
- **Seeking Alpha**—www.seekingalpha.com

- **Green Faucet**—www.greenfaucet.com
- **Morningstar**—www.morningstar.com

These sites not only offer stories pegged to the news events of the day, but also tell you about different ETFs, trends in the industry, and analysis on events currently impacting specific ETFs.

Analysis

In addition to staying on top of happenings in the stock market, you'll want sites that enable you to analyze ETFs for performance (including long and short funds, plus relative strength and weakness), holdings, expense ratios, trend lines, and so on.

Some of the ones I like best are these:

- **ETF Trends Analyzer** (www.etftrends.com)—Here you can do charting and view tables to see 50-day and 200-day moving averages. You can also view a comprehensive table that includes analysis on ETFs with $50 million or more in assets. This chart shows you daily and longer-term performance numbers, the yearly high, and what percentage above or below the trend lines a fund is.

- **ETF Connect** (www.etfconnect.com)—On ETF Connect, you can sort funds by characteristics such as premium, discount, current distribution rate, and size. You can also sort ETFs by asset class and sponsor. The site has interactive charting capabilities and portfolio trackers.

- **ETF Screen** (www.etfscreen.com)—ETF Screen delivers a great snapshot of what's moving day-to-day, updated every 15 minutes, as well as how funds have performed over the last five days, month, three months, six months, and year.

Looking Under the Hood

To learn more about ETFs, you'll also want to know things such as assets, trading volume, top holdings, and expense ratio. You can easily access this information at a number of sites.

The provider's site is the best place to gain all the information you could possibly need about an ETF. The names of all ETF providers are linked from the ETF provider's page on ETF Trends or will show up in any search engine search. Many providers also have very valuable education pages on their sites.

A couple of the notable ones include

- **PowerShares** (www.invescopowershares.com/resources/ investorguides)—Has several useful investor guides, and they also present exceptional educational webcasts.
- **iShares** (http://us.ishares.com/education_center/index. htm)—Has on-demand presentations and podcasts.
- **State Street Global Advisors** (www.spdru.com)—Has SPDR University, a valuable resource full of market commentary, webcasts, presentations, articles, and research papers. If you're a financial advisor, CD credits are available.
- **Morningstar** (www.morningstar.com)—Lists the top 25 holdings, their weighting within the fund, plus performance information, expense ratio, yield, assets, and more.
- **Yahoo! Finance** (www.finance.yahoo.com)—Lists the top ten holdings in a fund, plus yield, current headlines, expense ratio, assets, and more.

Charting

Many services offer charting tools, so you can more easily spot patterns, trends, and where funds are in relation to their trend lines:

- **ETF Trends** (www.etftrends.com)—On my site, you can see charting for any available ETF and can customize the view to your liking. If you want to see the 200-day moving average or a moving average in any other time frame, you can do so.

- **Yahoo! Finance** (www.finance.yahoo.com)—Yahoo! enables users to view both the SMA and EMA moving average, as well as both very short-term (five days) performance and up to 10 years of performance. It also has an interactive charting function that enables you to view a fund's all-time performance. You can set up a free portfolio and set sell points and monitor trend lines, as well.

- **Big Charts** (www.bigcharts.com)—Big Charts has detailed charting for all the major indexes and funds.

- **Stock Charts** (www.stockcharts.com)—Stock Charts has a number of charting capabilities: You can look at some of their free charts, or with a paid subscription, create your own chart and have it sent to your computer as an image file, and much more.

Many of these services are free to use, while others reserve their premium content for paid subscribers. I encourage you to look around and see what works best for you, but the sites mentioned above provide some of the best capabilities and information you'll find anywhere and enable you to become an informed investor.

chapter 7

Navigating U.S. Markets

When you're on the hunt for trends, one of the easiest ways to start is by looking at the major market indexes in the United States.

The Dow Jones Industrial Average (DJIA) is the barometer for the U.S. equity markets and is monitored daily by investors around the world. But the Dow is made up of only 30 stocks. While it's the best-known index, it's far from diversified. If you were looking for a better representation of U.S. stocks, you might pick the S&P 500, which is a large-cap value-weighted index, or the Russell 2000 index, which is a small-cap index.

There are many years when smaller companies perform better than large, established companies because they are more nimble and can better react to economic and market environments.

If you're leery of small companies, bear in mind that some of them won't always be small. Companies such as Microsoft (MSFT) and Home Depot (HD) were once small caps that were part of the Russell 2000 before they made it into the S&P 500 and eventually the Dow Jones Industrial Average.

But these indexes are only the beginning.

Broad indexes are great barometers for gauging the overall health of the markets. But if you only base your investments on the performance of the Dow, S&P 500, or Russell 2000, you're doing yourself and your portfolio a huge disservice.

If you need to invest in the stock market to reap growth, there are dozens of ways in which you can do it. The best place to start in this discussion is with the markets with which you are likely most familiar: the United States.

Choices Galore

As I noted in Chapter 2, "Risk and Disaster Don't Have to Go Hand-in-Hand," investors have been gravitating toward the most familiar benchmarks for decades. For the past 100 years, the most popular benchmarks by leaps and bounds have been the S&P 500 and the Dow. Investors tend to go with what makes them comfortable, what they know, and what they can easily check. The S&P, in particular, is the go-to index because of its diversity of holdings. The Dow, with only 30 holdings, is probably the most frequently talked about, but it's not the best barometer. There are a few major U.S. indexes (see Table 7.1), and they're all different in their construction.

Table 7.1 *The Major Indexes*

S&P 500	This value-weighted index, published since 1957, consists of 500 large-cap common stocks actively traded in the United States.
Dow	The oldest of the indexes, the Dow is computed from the prices of the 30 largest and most widely held public companies in the United States. It's market-value weighted, and the weighting percentage for these components adds up to 100%.
NASDAQ	The NASDAQ, started in 1971, holds 3,200 companies and is known for being a bellwether of the technology sector.
Russell 2000	The Russell 2000 is an index of 2,000 small-cap companies in the United States and is a subindex of the Russell 3000.

The universe of indexes goes way beyond the S&P 500 and Dow, however, covering all different sectors, subsectors, and asset classes. One reason so many indexes exist is that they all have a different take on the market, giving them their own unique performance at any given time.

For example, the large-cap S&P 500 could be trending higher, while the tech-heavy NASDAQ is trending lower. Or the small-cap Russell 2000 might be all the rage, while the 30 monsters in the Dow Jones are faltering.

As you can see from Figure 7.1, the NASDAQ Composite far outperformed the S&P 500 in the technology boom in the late 1990s.

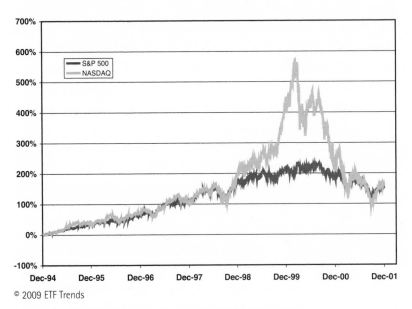

© 2009 ETF Trends

Figure 7.1 *S&P 500 versus NASDAQ Composite, 1994–2001*

Before talking more about certain periods of ups and downs for various indexes large and small, let's take an in-depth look at some of the most popular ones.

Dow Jones Industrial Average

The blue-chip Dow Jones 30 Industrial Average Index, started by journalist Charles Dow in 1896 (although it looks much different today), is the oldest and the best-known of the indexes run by

Dow Jones, Inc. Dow's creation was born from a desire to create a window through which stock market outsiders could peer in. While those on Wall Street were welcome to have a look, too, Dow wasn't as concerned with them. His index was for the common man—the Average Joe, if you will.

Today many other indexes exist, but the Dow is often considered the heartbeat of the American economy. Any given day after the markets close, we can hold up our stethoscopes and listen with bated breath as the business reporters on television and in newspapers give us a number. For many people, right or not, the Dow *is* the stock market.

In some ways, the Dow doesn't look much like it did in those early days. In the beginning, it had an unweighted average of 11 companies. In 1928, it was finally expanded to 30 large-cap stocks—companies with a market capitalization of at least $10 billion, although this can change over time—representing every major sector in the stock market.

Whatever path a company is taking to get to the upper echelon, one thing is for certain: As long as the stock price continues to rise, so does the company's market cap. Most large-caps are in the energy, technology, financial, and healthcare sectors, reflecting those sectors' growing importance and relevance in our economy. The financial and healthcare sectors are particularly catering to baby boomers, as their generation ages.

Large-caps are generally best suited for a long-term investment because these big companies aren't growing at a rate as fast as small-caps and mid-caps. After all, when you're at the top, you don't have as much room to grow. But in exchange for the slower but steady growth, your money buys you a measure of security.

The current components of the Dow Jones Industrial Average are some of the most common, best-known, and largest companies operating in the United States today (see Table 7.2).

Table 7.2 *The Current Dow 30 **

3M	Exxon	Merck
Alcoa Inc.	General Electric	Microsoft
American Express	General Motors	Pfizer
AT&T	Hewlett-Packard	The Coca-Cola Company
Bank of America	Intel	The Home Depot
Boeing Co.	IBM	The Procter & Gamble Co.
Caterpillar Inc.	Johnson & Johnson	United Technologies
Chevron	JPMorgan Chase	Verizon
Citigroup	Kraft Foods	Wal-Mart
duPont	McDonald's	Walt Disney

*As of March 2009

The S&P 500

Introduced in 1957, the Standard & Poor's 500 is a compendium of the 500 largest publicly owned corporations, most of which are American. The companies in this index are chosen by committee and are broadly representative of the various industries in the U.S. economy.

The S&P 500 isn't as simple as it looks, though. This index isn't merely a list of the 500 largest corporations. It is a market-weighted index, and companies gain entrance based on a variety of factors: market size, liquidity (the ability to buy or sell an asset in large quantities without doing a number on the asset's price), and how well they represent their sector overall.

Russell Mid-Cap Index

Mid-cap stocks are those with a market cap between $1 billion and $8 billion. Although the companies that make up the large-caps in the United States are mostly household names, mid-caps aren't firmly defined. According to Morningstar, "The best way to get a handle on the mid-cap universe is to view it as a collection of the most successful small-cap stocks and the least successful large-cap stocks."

An added bonus of mid-caps is greater transparency: Small and medium-sized companies tend to have financial statements that read much simpler than those of large-caps. Before you write off mid-caps as too "middle," consider this: Home Depot (HD), the world's largest home improvement retailer, was once a mid-cap. Most of the big companies we know today had to start somewhere. Today Home Depot operates more than 2,000 stores in the United States, Canada, Mexico, and China, and enjoys a position in the Dow Jones Industrial Average. When you invest in today's mid-caps, you just might be sitting on tomorrow's large-caps.

The Russell 2000

The Russell 2000 Index measures the performance of the small-cap segment of the U.S. equity universe. It includes approximately 2,000 of the smallest securities, based on a combination of market cap and current index membership.

Small-caps are companies with a market capitalization between $250 million and $2 billion. Small-caps have a number of pros and cons: First, they have tremendous growth potential. Everyone has to start somewhere, right? Most companies don't burst onto the scene, brimming with assets. These types of companies help fuel the Russell 2000 to outperform the large-cap index during the long-term uptrends.

Large-caps might be the squeaky wheels that get the grease, but don't be so quick to dismiss the lesser-known entities. Small-caps and mid-caps outperformed large-caps between 1998 and 2007. In all but one year, from 1926 to 2006, small-company stocks outperformed the largest stocks, according to a study by Ibbotson Associates. The study also revealed that $1 invested each in small-cap and large-cap equities in 1926 would be valued at $15,921 and $3,077, respectively, as of December 31, 2006.

In fact, after the 15 bear markets since 1932, small-caps outperformed large-caps 12 times, according to research from The Leuthold Group, a Minneapolis-based firm. For example, in the 12 months following the 2000–2002 bear market, small-cap performance nearly doubled that of large-caps, 46% versus 24%. Another illustration of this wide gap came a year following the 1982 crash, when small-caps surged 96% compared to 59% for their large-cap counterparts.

SMALL-CAPS SHINE AFTER RECESSION

In late 2008, the National Bureau of Economic Research (NBER) officially announced that the U.S. economy was in a recession. Interestingly, whether you consider one month, six months, one year, or even three years after a recession, small-cap stocks trounce their larger brethren coming out of slowdowns, according to the data crunchers at *Old Mutual* and *Morningstar.*

Why is this? Small-caps are nimble and quick to react to changing market conditions. They also don't have the issues with bureaucracy that larger companies can, potentially inhibiting bold moves.

Growth Versus Value

A question as old as the stock market itself is, "Should I invest in growth or value stocks?" This question can apply to both global and domestic markets, but I discuss it here because the debate tends to center more on domestic companies.

Growth companies are those that are important to our economic growth, such as technology. If these companies catch on, they'll sprint right to the front of the line with a cutting-edge product or business model.

Their price-to-earnings ratio (P/E) is often substantially higher than average, but it's worth it when you think about where the company might be in a few years. The price-to-earnings (P/E) ratio is the valuation ratio of a company's current share price compared to its earnings per share. A high P/E ratio can often suggest that investors are expecting a higher earnings growth in the future. High-growth-oriented companies tend to have higher P/E ratios because their price is reflected in the anticipation of future earnings.

Growth is like an action flick: all thrills and big explosions. It's exciting, it's heady, and you don't know what's going to happen next.

Value: Slower but Steadier

Value is like a documentary: It's steadier, calmer, more collected, and more reasoned. It's definitely not as exciting, but it might be more rewarding in the long run. A value investor looks for companies that have proven themselves or their products. Consider the biotechnology industry, for example. Many of the smaller biotechnology firms don't even make money at this stage because they are still conducting heavy research and clinical trials, waiting for their "big break." A true value investor would never invest in a company that does not make money, even if the potential for reward down the line might be greater.

If you're a value investor, you want to see that the company is making money and that the stock is inexpensive relative to the future earnings of the company. Many ways of determining this exist, but perhaps the most widely used method is looking at the P/E ratio of the company.

More consistent earnings with companies with lower P/E ratios would point to attractive value stocks.

Trends in Value and Growth

The growth versus value debate refuses to go away. It's worth noting that those who choose the growth approach consistently underperform the market. In the last 20 years, the S&P 500 has obtained compound annual returns of 13% per year. Also in the last 20 years, small-cap companies (smaller than $2 billion) that were considered growth companies obtained compound annual returns of 8.8%, worse than all other types and more than 40% less than that of value investment returns of 15%.

Interestingly, during bear markets, value stocks tend to make money while nearly everything else around them crumbles. Consider the 2000–2002 bear market, for example. As measured by the dividend-adjusted version of the Dow Jones Wilshire 5000 index, the overall stock market declined by 48.6%.

On the other hand, according to data compiled by University of Chicago finance professor Eugene Fama and Dartmouth University finance professor Kenneth French, the average value stock over this time gained more than 80%.

That's not the only time this has happened. During the 1972–1974 bear market, the Dow Jones Wilshire 5000 index lost 42%, while value stocks gained nearly 40%.

Although both growth and value have their merits, the important thing to understand is that they tend to operate on their own individual trends.

The best strategy is to let the market tell you where to go when it comes to asset classes. Coming out of the 2000–2002 bear market, you can look back and find that small-cap growth was the best performer, and use that as a basis for where to look when coming out of future bears.

But what works best looking at the trend line. Look at those areas that are first to move above their 200-day moving averages when emerging from a bear. Those that develop an uptrend earlier tend to be the best performers when there's a long-term uptrend.

Domestic Market ETFs

Some of the most basic ETFs are based on well-known stock indexes. These are also some of the most popular and heavily traded ETFs. This has much to do with a few factors, including name recognition and the fact that these ETFs can make a great centerpiece for a portfolio that needs a little domestic representation.

Depending on which fund you choose, you can get a well-diversified cross-section of the U.S. markets—or in the case of the NASDAQ, a good cross-section of the technology sector. The four of the most popular and heavily traded of these ETFs include these:

- **The SPDRS (SPY)** (www.spdrs.com)—Tracks the S&P 500 Index. Its top holdings include Exxon (XOM), Johnson & Johnson (JNJ), AT&T (T), and Procter & Gamble (PG).

- **The Diamonds (DIA), by SSGA** (www.ssgafunds.com)—
  Tracks the Dow Jones Industrial Average. Its top holdings
  include IBM (IBM), Exxon (XOM), Chevron (CVX), and
  Johnson & Johnson (JNJ).

- **The Cubes (QQQQ), by PowerShares** (www.invesco
  powershares.com)—Tracks the NASDAQ. Top holdings
  include Apple (APPL), Qualcomm (QCOM), Microsoft
  (MSFT), and Google (GOOG).

- **iShares Russell 2000 Index (IWM)** (www.ishares.
  com)—Tracks the Russell 2000 Index of small-caps. Its top
  holdings include Myriad Genetics (MYGN), Ralcorp
  Holdings (RAH), Alexion Pharmaceuticals (ALXN), and
  Sybase Inc. (SY).

Digging in Even Deeper

If you need a great, simple core holding, you can look at these funds
for some ideas. But if you want to break it down further, you have
even more options to do so. From this point, you can find ETFs that
segment their underlying indexes even further, breaking them up into
large-cap, mid-cap, and small-cap, or separating them into growth
versus value.

This is where ETFs really come in handy, too—as you break up
the markets into segments, you might begin to see more obscure
names popping up as you research companies. Or there might be
other companies that are gems you would have had a hard time dis-
covering on your own. If you were picking individual stocks, you'd
have to do a lot of research that might not be easy to come by. The
builders of these indexes underlying ETFs have already done that
heavy lifting for you.

As I mentioned earlier, different segments of the market tend to operate on their own trend lines and do well in different economic environments. With ETFs, it's easy to carve out these areas and give your portfolio the level of exposure you want.

- **MidCap SPDRS (MDY)** (www.spdrs.com)—Tracks the S&P MidCap 400 Index. Top holdings include Vertex Pharmaceuticals (VRTX), New York Community Bancorp (NYB), Quanta Services (PWR), and SAIC, Inc. (SAI).

- **iShares Russell 1000 Growth Index (IWF)** (www.ishares.com)—Tracks the Russell 1000 Growth Index. Its top components include Microsoft (MSFT), IBM (IBM), Cisco (CSCO), and Wal-Mart (WMT).

- **Vanguard Value (VTV)** (www.vanguard.com)—Tracks the MSCI US Prime Market Value Index. Among the top components are ExxonMobil (XOM), General Electric (GE), AT&T (T), and Chevron (CVX).

Domestic ETFs come in all types—growth, value, and a blend of both; they can also cover large-caps, mid-caps, or small-caps. There's no need to stop there, though. You can break it down even further, with funds such as iShares S&P MidCap Growth (IJK), Vanguard Small Cap Growth (VBK), PowerShares Zacks Micro Cap (PZI), and the First Trust Dow Jones Select MicroCap (FDM).

chapter 8

International Opportunities

Countries around the world have had their share of economic prosperity and challenges that spill into both domestic and global markets. Peaks and valleys, expansions, and recessions are usually clearly defined and cyclical in nature.

You eliminate or minimize exposure to these countries in your portfolio to your own detriment, though, because nearly 70% of the global market capitalization is outside the United States. The United States still has a major portion, but both developed and emerging markets are increasingly seeking their piece of the pie.

Trade, currency, and economic issues all affect companies in different ways. Over time, countries encounter both challenges and opportunities that have positive as well as negative effects on their markets. Rarely do all countries and global regions enjoy prosperity at the same time and economic challenges at the same time. By identifying countries that are prospering during periods when their markets are trending in the right direction, investors have opportunities to diversify their portfolios and profit outside domestic markets.

As a result, some countries can be thriving while others are struggling. An increasingly global economy has made many countries dependent on one another in some way. That being said, opportunities can be found in all corners of the world, whether in a country that's firmly established and operating or a country that's just gaining access to the technologies that will help it to grow.

In 2008, the United States had 29.9% of the global market cap, down sharply from the 43.7% it enjoyed in 2004. We can expect to see this number continue to shrink as more countries emerge and become serious players. Japan is second, at 8.2%; the United Kingdom has 6.8%; and China, an emerging market, has 5.4%. Other countries have a very small percentage of the global market cap—for example, Saudi Arabia had 0.9% in 2008. However, that's an 877.5% increase since 2004. Egypt had 0.2% in 2008, up 561.6% since 2004. This should tell you two things: The United States is not ruling the global economy as much as it once was, and other countries are growing at a blistering pace.

The argument between whether one should invest in a developed market or a frontier market resembles the "growth versus value" debate that I discussed in Chapter 7, "Navigating U.S. Markets." Developed markets are already established and thriving, and they probably won't get much more powerful than they already are. However, frontier markets are starting at practically ground zero. If they are successful, they could deliver outsize returns.

Global markets offer investors the chance to access growth in other areas when domestic markets are weak. With some exceptions (most notably, the 2008 crisis), when things were solid in the United States, global markets were thriving, too. In 2005, returns in foreign developed markets in Asia, Latin America, and Europe soared and outperformed domestic markets, as shown in Table 8.1.

Table 8.1   *Returns of Various Markets in 2005*

United States	5.4%
Britain	14.1%
Canada	22%
Japan	36.9%
France	23.8%
Germany	22.9%
Hong Kong	4.2%
Switzerland	31.5%
Australia	17.1%

To invest in foreign markets, you can carve out regional markets and country-specific markets that operate on their own individual trends. For a stark example of this, we need look no further than Japan.

The Land of the Rising Sun...and Profits

Japan's economy hit its stride in 1982, just as stagnating 15% interest rates ushered in a recession in the United States. It was definitely a tale of two economies.

At that time, productivity by Japan's baby boomer generation was unprecedented, and inflation was nearly nil, from lingering conservation efforts during the oil shock of the 1970s. Japan was the talk and envy of the globe, with a work ethic and an electronic explosion that were second to none. Toyota (TM) launched its Camry in 1982 and sold more than 12 million cars, to become a major financial powerhouse. While the United States was becoming a debtor nation, Japan became the world's largest creditor. Its financial and banking industries grew uncontrollably in the remainder of the 1980s.

In the investment world, the Tokyo Securities and Stock Exchange developed into the largest in the world in 1988 in terms of combined market value and capitalization. Stock market trading exploded and stock prices rose rapidly. The trading recorded by the Nikkei stock average, compiled by the *Japan Economic Daily*, grew from 6,850 in October 1982, to nearly 39,000 in early 1990. During one six-month period in 1986, total trade volume on the Tokyo exchange increased by 250%.

The Nikkei gained nearly 4,700% in an eight-year span, a spectacular run that you can see in Figure 8.1. The United States suffered a recession in 1980–1982 and then dealt with the Crash of 1987.

© 2009 ETF Trends

Figure 8.1 *Nikkei Index, 1984–2009*

The Beginning of the End

December 29, 1989, spelled the beginning of the end for Japan's bull run. That day, the Nikkei 225 peaked at 38,915.87, fueled by a run-up in corporate debt and property values (much like what happened to the United States in 2007–2008).

Consider these details, from *Japan: A Country Study*, a book edited by Ronald E. Dolan (1992, Government Printing Office):

"A penthouse apartment in Tokyo might rent for $10 million—dollars, not yen—a month. In a drive for ever greater productivity, wages had stagnated and workers routinely put in 15-hour days just to keep pace with their income of three years earlier."

By now, it's a very familiar tale. Between 1986 and 1988, the price of commercial land in greater Tokyo doubled. Real estate prices soared so much that "Tokyo alone was worth more than the United States." Between 1955 and 1990, land prices in Japan appreciated by 70 times and stocks increased 100 times over. An average home near Tokyo cost more than $2 million in 1989. Large-scale stock speculation went global as the world clamored for Japanese shares. These euphoric investors believed in a perpetual bull market. The newly wealthy bought luxury goods and lived well beyond their means. Many point to inflated values, false hopes, and hype as the reason for the Nikkei's climb—not solid financials.

Unfortunately, all excessively good things must end. To cool the inflated economy, the Japanese government raised interest rates. Over a period of years, the Nikkei stock index crashed by more than 30,000 points. In Figure 8.2, you can see where you would have protected yourself.

When the Nikkei finally crumbled, it lost two-thirds of its value, to 14,000, over the next eight months. Japanese housing prices plummeted for 14 consecutive years. Many compare its severity to the U.S. market crash and depression in 1929. Yet unlike its Western market counterparts, the Nikkei remained flat for the next 17 years before diving another 47% in 2008.

As we know through monitoring trends, no market is protected from huge market swings. If you had known this, you would have participated in the uptrend and avoided the downtrend.

© 2009 ETF Trends

Figure 8.2 *Nikkei with 200-day moving average, 1984–2009*

Emerging Markets

You can't blame investors for being drawn to international investments. As technology and money spreads around the world, it gives
once far-flung and removed economies a chance to participate in a
global boom.

Emerging markets have offered tremendous profits (and
headaches) over the years. They're attractive because, as much as
they're growing, and as rapidly as they're growing, they've got even
more room to expand. Popularity in overseas investments especially
surges when things on the home front aren't so sweet and profits in
other countries are. But to consider these areas of the world as only
"fair-weather friends" is folly because they have a lot to offer in any
kind of climate.

What is an emerging market? Definitions tend to vary, but often emerging markets are considered such because of their developments and reforms. China, an economic powerhouse, is still lumped into the emerging category because it's still working on reforms and policies. China is a country very much in transition, a hallmark of any emerging economy. You're probably not going to see Britain making too many drastic changes to its economic policies, but this kind of thing is *de rigueur* in emerging markets.

Among the best-known emerging markets are the BRICs, a group of four powerhouse economies: Brazil, Russia, India, and China. The name emerged from a Goldman Sachs report in 2003 that speculated that, by 2050, these four economies would be wealthier than most major economic powers.

Smaller than emerging markets are frontier markets, which occupy the farthest reaches of the emerging-markets universe. Countries such as Vietnam, Thailand, and Zimbabwe occupy this space. These world markets are often in a state of political upheaval, often with sky-high inflation, very weak currencies, and markets that are heavily subject to local whims and prejudices. They offer high reward potential, but as you know by now, that comes with high risk.

From 2002 to 2007, the average diversified emerging markets stock fund gained about 25% annually. Comparatively, the Dow Jones Industrial Average returned around 5% a year during this same stretch. And in 2006, when the S&P chalked up 15.8%, emerging markets equities generated nearly twice those gains (see Table 8.2). Before that period, emerging markets were a little topsy-turvy, as shown in Figure 8.3.

Table 8.2   *Best-Performing Emerging Markets, 2004–2007*

Region	3-Year Gains, Annualized
Latin America	39.5%
Eastern Europe	34.6%
BRIC (Brazil, Russia, India, and China)	33.0%
Middle East	27.0%
Asia	18.8%
Overall emerging markets	24.9%

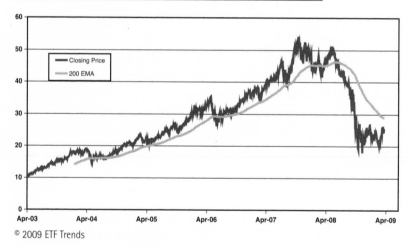

© 2009 ETF Trends

Figure 8.3   *iShares MSCI Emerging Markets (EEM) with 200-day moving average, 2003–2009*

China's Dragon

Previously, investors might have had many reasons and excuses for discounting or ignoring emerging and frontier markets. This is no longer the case, however. To deny these countries a space in your portfolio is to miss out on periods of growth as seen earlier in China. With the tools available to investors, today it's easier than ever to safely access these markets. One of the easiest ways to invest in these areas is with ETFs. By using a trend following strategy with these funds, investors could have had the opportunity to capture some of the growth China saw in the 2000s, as shown in Figure 8.4. Let's see how.

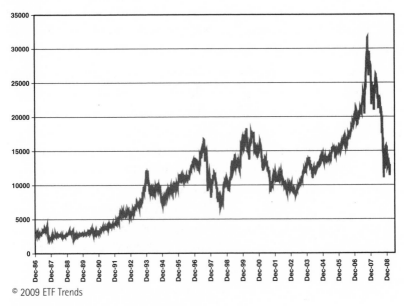

© 2009 ETF Trends

Figure 8.4 *Hang Seng Index, 1986–2008*

As in the technology boom, people thought you could throw a dart at an international stock board and make triple-digit gains. Trouble is, the extreme volatility of emerging-markets funds, especially those that focus on Asia, often provokes investors to sell at the wrong times—and lures them into buying at the wrong times, too. China is a perfect example.

China's story is really one of rags to riches. When President Jimmy Carter normalized diplomatic relations with the Chinese three decades ago, paving the way to an unimpeded flow of exports, we're pretty sure he had no idea that the Red Dragon's unleashing would become such a beast and blessing for Americans.

In slightly more than a quarter-century, China has transformed itself from an impoverished and closed agricultural society to a globally integrated industrial powerhouse. At its peak, China's gross domestic product grew at 11% annually, spending trillions of dollars revamping a crumbling infrastructure and modernizing its transportation systems. Later China went on an unprecedented pre-Olympic spending spree—which might have been a case of too much, too soon.

China's stock market peaked in October 2007, nearly quadrupling over five years. Investors who bought stock in companies that fed the Red Dragon (oil, food, building materials, and so on) made handsome profits. Those who entered the positions without a sell discipline learned a harsh lesson. By early 2008, China's market and economy began to fall. China suffered from fuel shortages; transportation disruptions, slowing real estate values; and the threat of social unrest from farmers protesting over land seizures and from airline workers striking. As a result, the largest China ETF, iShares FTSE/Xinhua China 25 Index FXI (you can compare it to the U.S. DJIA) toppled 65.8% from its October 2007 all-time high.

As you can see from Figure 8.5, if you were monitoring the 200-day moving average of the FXI, you could easily have ridden the trend and exited when it went below its 200-day in early January 2008.

Investing in Emerging Economies

The benefits of using a trend following strategy to access the fits and starts of emerging markets should be clear by now. No emerging economy is on a steady growth path, which is why the strategy makes even more sense here. You can use it to spot waves as they appear and to hop off as they peter out. Emerging markets are just that: emerging. For that reason, they provide opportunities not seen in developed markets.

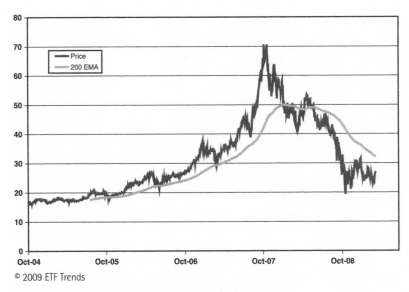

© 2009 ETF Trends

Figure 8.5 *iShares FTSE/Xinhua China 25 (FXI), 2004–2008*

They tend to be more volatile, there's more potential on the upside, and, as you can see in the example of China, the downside can be even more devastating. Having an entry and exit strategy can help get you in and out of these exciting markets at more desirable times.

Another BRIC in the Wall

In particular, countries such as the so-called BRICs (Brazil, Russia, India, and China) were among the top performers from 2003 to 2007. Some funds that focused on these areas delivered returns of 70% or more. But 2008 dawned and delivered a rude awakening as a global slowdown and credit crisis trickled into seemingly every corner of the world.

Many investors and analysts believed these economies were so strong that decoupling was not far in the future. But recent history has shown that all countries are intertwined. The United States depends on these countries for their imports, and they depend on us to buy their goods. Skyrocketing oil prices, tight lending, and a shrinking pool of disposable income hit some of these economies right in the solar plexus in 2008.

The good news is that although these economies have been hit just as hard as the rest of the world by the market turmoil, investors who missed the boat have a golden opportunity to get in at lower prices. This can be done easily if there's a strategy in place. Investors would be unwise to turn their backs on a global region while it's down and out. Instead, these areas are worth watching: As in any other depressed area, a turnaround will take place, and you won't want to miss it.

The BRICs, particularly China and India, are being eyed with great interest around the world. Some feel that these economies could give the United States a run for its money some day, with their vast amounts of intellectual capital and room for explosive growth.

International ETFs

International ETFs are among the most popular and versatile funds in the ETF arena. Depending on the level of exposure you'd like, you have a number of choices: regions, countries within a region or group (think BRICs), or a single country.

Whether you want exposure to an established market or one in its infancy, you can use ETFs in two common ways:

- Target a specific emerging market with a single-country fund, which can potentially deliver higher volatility but greater rewards when that country does well.
- Choose a region or class of emerging markets with a broad-based fund, which spreads the risk and volatility over several emerging-market countries.

Developed Markets

Developed-market ETFs can help provide some stability to an ETF portfolio. As I've said, these countries are well established and aren't looking for explosive growth. But on the flip-side, catastrophic declines are unlikely, making their risk lower than that of a frontier market fund.

The fund types are similar to that of emerging markets: all-encompassing funds, regional funds, and single-country funds. One of the broadest funds available is the BLDRS Developed Markets 100 ADR (ADRD) (www.adrbnymellon.com/bldrs_overview.jsp), which has weightings in the United Kingdom, Japan, France, and Switzerland. The Claymore/Zacks Country Rotation (CRO) (www.claymore.com) is made up of 200 stocks selected from a universe of international companies listed on developed international exchanges. Country exposure includes Australia, Singapore, Spain, and Sweden.

Funds with more regional developed market exposure include these:

- **iShares S&P Europe 350 (IEV)**—Tracks the S&P Europe 350 Index. Its top country weightings are the United Kingdom, France, and Switzerland. (www.ishares.com)

- **PowerShares Dynamic Europe (PEH)**—Tracks the QSG Active Europe Index. Its top country weightings are the United Kingdom, France, and Italy. (www.invescopowershares.com)

As with emerging market ETFs, some funds provide access to a range of developed markets, including these:

- **iShares MSCI Japan (EWJ)**—Tracks the MSCI Japan Index. Its top holdings include Toyota, Mitsubishi, and Takeda Pharmaceutical.

- **iShares MSCI Canada (EWC)**—Tracks the MSCI Canada Index. Its top holdings include Encana Corp (ECA), Royal Bank of Canada (RY), and Barrick Gold (ABX).
- **iShares MSCI Australia (EWA)**—Tracks the MSCI Australia Index. Its top holdings include BHP Billiton, Westpac, and Commonwealth Bank of Australia.

Emerging Markets

One of the simplest ways to access emerging markets is through all-encompassing ETFs such as the iShares Emerging Markets Index (EEM), which delivers exposure to countries such as Brazil, Taiwan, South Korea, South Africa, Israel, Turkey, Hungary, and China.

If you'd like to target a region, you can do this with funds such as the WisdomTree Middle East Dividend (GULF) (www.wisdomtree.com), SPDR S&P Emerging Europe (GUR) (www.spdretfs.com), PowerShares MENA Frontier Countries (PMNA), or SPDR S&P Emerging Asia Pacific (GMF).

The BRIC region has several ETFs available for investors to gain exposure. Among the most popular BRIC ETFs are these:

- **Claymore/BNY BRIC (EEB)**—Tracks the New York BRIC Select ADR Index. Its top holdings include China Mobile Limited (CHL), Companhia Vale (RIO), and Brazilian Petroleum Corporation. (www.claymore.com)
- **SPDR S&P BRIC (BIK)**—Tracks the S&P BRIC 40 Index. Its top holdings include China Mobile, Gazprom, and Brazilian Petroleum.
- **iShares MSCI BRIC (BKF)**—Tracks the MSCI BRIC Index. Its top holdings include China Mobile, Gazprom, and China Life Insurance.

How do you choose a fund? If you look under the hood, you'll see that countries within each fund have different weightings. If you'd like more access to, say, China, you might be interested in BIK because it states a 42.8% weighting. If you'd like more Brazil, you'd be interested in EEB, which has a 49.4% weighting for that country.

If you really want to focus on a single emerging market, dozens of funds are available to do this, including these:

- **Market Vectors Russia (RSX)**—Tracks the DAXglobal Russia+ Index. Its top holdings include Mobile Telsys, Surgutneftegas, and Vimpel. (www.vaneck.com)

- **iShares MSCI Thailand (THD)**—Tracks the MSCI Thailand Index. Its top holdings include Bangkok Bank, Siam Cemebt, and Kasikornbank.

- **iShares MSCI Israel (EIS)**—Tracks the MSCI Israel Index. Its top holdings include Check Point Software Technology, Israel Chemicals, and Teva Pharmaceutical.

- **Market Vectors Indonesia (IDX)**—Tracks the Market Vectors Indonesia Index. Its top holdings include Bank Mandiri, Bank Rakyat Indonesia, and Unilever Indonesia.

chapter 9

The Best-Looking Sector
in the Room

There are now so many sectors available to you as an investor, and the market has been sliced and diced to give you more choice and opportunity than ever before. Some have been critics of the level of slicing and dicing, but when investors have choices and options, it keeps competition healthy. And today's technology has given us the tools we need to do the proper research and watch trends develop in real time.

Check under the broad market umbrella, and you'll find literally thousands of subsectors with trends (and minds) of their own. Maybe the Dow is down, but healthcare, or even more specifically, medical devices, might be riding a huge bull wave.

Trends in subsectors can run contrary to the broader market. In other words, you could stand to make money instead of lose it in down markets or make a whole lot more money in up markets by investing in subsector trends.

These subsectors provide huge profit opportunities regardless of the broad market climate. I'm talking about opportunities in every nook and cranny of the markets—emerging countries, economic powerhouses, commodities, currencies, semiconductors, utilities, telecommunications, transportation, and a whole lot more.

The market is made up of thousands of moving parts. Some are working together, some oppose each other, others are off in their own little world, moving any which way they feel.

The U.S. economy and the various sectors comprising it are not immune from cycles of boom and bust. The spectacular growth and even more spectacular collapse of the technology sector is a major example.

But many sectors in the United States often move along on their own trends. While some companies are focusing on healthcare and making better drugs, the utility sector might be suffering under the weight of our nation's aging and rickety power grid. Or as patents in the pharmaceutical sector are expiring, a new solar company has come forth with the latest and greatest panel.

A number of sectors make up the U.S. economy, including aerospace and defense, transportation, media, healthcare, utilities, finance, and engineering. Investors who want to drill down even further can get into subsectors, such as regional banks, biotechnology, airlines, pharmaceuticals, water, and more. Opportunities to get into sectors abound, and many operate independently of one another. For example, healthcare and transportation are marching to the beat of their own drummers. If one sector is transitioning out of an uptrend, you can no doubt find another sector just entering into one.

With ETFs, investors can access all of these areas. It's just a matter of how specialized you want to get. Accessing a broad sector such as utilities will deliver a little more stability. But if you choose to invest in wind technologies, you might see more drastic movements.

One issue that often comes up when discussing sectors is that of cyclical investing. This often involves identifying companies or sectors that tend to do well in certain periods of the markets. Automobile companies, steel, and fine dining are types of companies that tend to follow in lockstep with the broader economy. As the economy booms, the auto and restaurant industries tend to be beneficiaries. On the downside, this can make them vulnerable in recessionary periods.

Some investors might experience success with cyclical investing, and while there are merits to it, I feel that trend following is a better way to capture these movements because it doesn't involve predicting market upswings (or downswings). As you have probably often seen, the market isn't always perfectly predictable, which is why listening to the messages that it's sending will benefit you more in the long run than trying to guess what it's going to tell you ahead of time.

In the past two decades, one of the most exciting sectors in the world has been technology. Many Americans today have watched the computer evolve from a massive machine that took up an entire room to something they can fit in their pockets. Millions of people around the world want information right at their fingertips, and companies are positioned to create billions' worth of value.

But this growth hasn't come without some hiccups and volatility, as people figure out what this industry means to them and the world. As an example, we need to look no further than the 1990s.

Technology: High Highs and Lower Lows

The U.S. military created the Internet decades before "dotcom" became a household name. It vastly underestimated the numbers and enthusiasm of people wanting to go online. By 1995, the Internet caught on like wildfire, with an estimated 18 million users. Soon speculators were barely able to control their excitement over this new economy: The Internet seemed like one technology that wouldn't be disappearing anytime soon. No wonder everyone believed it was a "can't lose" bet.

Technology became the sexiest and most profitable investment game in town. You couldn't swing a stick without hearing about some kid who had millions in stock options at his hot new tech job. At the height of the bubble, a new IT company could raise significant amounts of money through its initial public offering (IPO), even though its coffers had run dry or, in some instances, had never made a penny.

Investors wanted to believe that they could be making all that money, too. They stepped into the market, ignored the state of companies' balance sheets, and bought stocks on the promise of growing demand for IT products and future profits. Although "fundamentals" aren't the be-all, end-all, they shouldn't be disregarded, either. This kind of information about tech companies could have kept investors on guard for a fall.

Greed soon kicked in. Early in the frenzy, in December 1996, former Fed chairman Alan Greenspan uttered his famous "irrational exuberance" phrase to describe the mania enveloping technology stocks. Investors simply bought anything with a dotcom label attached to it. Pets.com. Webvan.com. The dotcom graveyard is vast.

In October 1990, the tech-laden NASDAQ Index was a low of nearly 300. By March 2000, it reached a high of just above 5,000—an increase of 1,456%. The index gained 86% in 1999 alone. After 1997, technology improvements kept coming and productivity kept rising. Profits, however, did not.

The Bubble Springs a Leak

The madness continued unabated for several years, until finally cracks began to appear. Companies themselves poked the first holes in this bubble: Many reported huge losses and some folded outright within months of their IPO. In 1999, there were 457 IPOs, most of which were related to Internet and technology. Of those 457 IPOs, 117 doubled in price on the first day of trading.

The mania was apparent in the performance of two major indexes. Figure 9.1 shows how the NASDAQ Composite and Dow rose sharply in this time period.

From its high of 5,048 reached on March 10, 2000, to its low of 1,114 hit on October 9, 2002, the NASDAQ Composite lost 78% of its value, as shown in Figure 9.2.

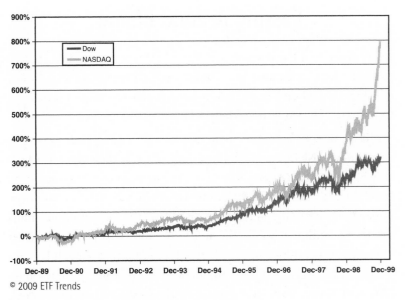

© 2009 ETF Trends

Figure 9.1   *Dow and NASDAQ Composite, 1990s*

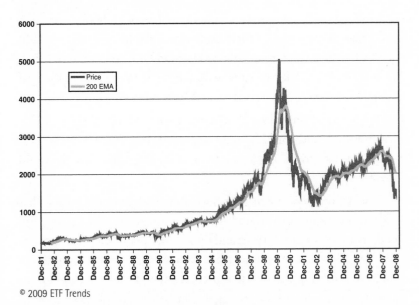

© 2009 ETF Trends

Figure 9.2   *NASDAQ Composite, 1982–2008*

Passing Around Blame

Many argue that the dotcom boom and bust was a case of too much, too fast. Companies unable to decide on their corporate creed were given millions of dollars and told to grow to mammoth proportions by tomorrow. This was a time when nearly anything seemed possible.

Remember what I said about investors becoming more willing to accept more risk in the good times? Talk of triple-digit gains and how easy it was to make money lured even the most conservative investors from their secure S&P 500 positions. Feeling regret in 1999 over missing one-year triple-digit gains in blue-chip stock positions, hundreds of millions were flowing into funds such as Invesco Telecommunications and Fidelity Technology. Meanwhile, the Vanguard 500 S&P 500 fund experienced the first net outflows in its history in March 2000—the same time the NASDAQ hit its 52-week high of 5,048.

Unfortunately, those who bought tech stocks hook, line, and sinker have had to pay for their exuberance. An investor who bought the NASDAQ at the top in early 2000 would have recovered only half his losses today. What happened with the NASDAQ is one of the best examples of the cracks in the buy-and-hold philosophy.

It's never wrong to catch a moving wave. Technology was in a clear uptrend, and you can't fight the trend. But investors must protect themselves by having a plan to head for the exits when the trend is losing steam.

The technology boom and bust illustrates another fallacy that tends to make its way around the investing world when things are good: that this will last forever and those other boom–bust cycles were different. How much investors buy into that often determines how much trouble they'll have when it comes time to let go. I'm here to tell you that pushing those thoughts out of your head now will save you much pain and heartache later, because it is never different and never will be.

"People are starting to say that buy-and-hold didn't work too well," says investor Bill Fritz. "I think that it's the reason I like the strategy, that it should be a nonemotional decision of when to get in and when to get out. I didn't take a hit in '87, I didn't take a hit in 2000, and I didn't take a hit in 2008."

An argument buy-and-holders frequently make is that the markets tend to go up in the long term, but anyone who has held on to the NAS-DAQ in hopes of recovering what was lost is still waiting. The NASDAQ has never again come close to its 2000 highs.

One Big Financial Mess

You can think of the financial crisis of 2008 as a snowball that started small and grew to iceberg proportions in very little time. It pushed the United States into a recession and sent major stock indexes spiraling to their lowest points in decades.

It all started with the real estate glut of the 2000s and the greed of wannabe homeowners and loose lending standards. Americans were given subprime mortgage loans regardless of credit history, income, or ability to pay. These variable loans attracted buyers with very low interest rates for the first few years; then mortgages jumped, often doubling, when that initial period ended.

This is an oversimplification of a very big problem, though. Also in the mix were complicated investment tools such as credit default swaps (CDS) and collateralized debt obligations (CDO) that, when finally revealed to the public at large, showed the cracks and flaws in a system that had gotten too big to support itself.

One of the largest financial services ETFs, the iShares Dow Jones U.S. Financial Sector (IYF) (www.ishares.com), shows the slow rise to the peak, followed by a precipitous fall, as shown in Figure 9.3. It holds some of the country's largest banks and financial institutions, including American Express (AXP), Bank of America (BAC), and JPMorgan Chase (JPM).

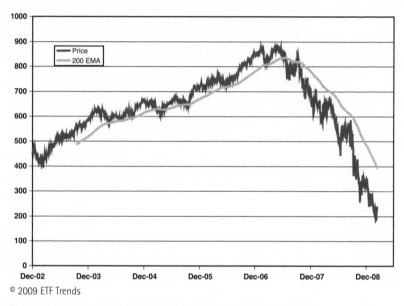

© 2009 ETF Trends

Figure 9.3 *Dow Jones U.S. Financial Sector Index, 2002–2008*

Unable to keep up with rising mortgages, delinquencies and fore-closures in the United States began popping up at an unprecedented pace. By September 2008, we witnessed the failure and merging of a number of banks and lending institutions. Once the wall started to fall, momentum picked up and knocked down companies we thought would stand the test of time. We were wrong.

The Beginning of the Global Crisis

Numerous plans were put forward with intent to solve the crisis. In the end, then-President George W. Bush and Secretary of the

Treasury Henry Paulson announced a $700 billion financial aid package in September 2008, intended to limit the damage that the events in weeks prior to that caused. Banks announced new writedowns seemingly every single day. Economic indicators popped up all over the place signaling that there was real trouble. Job losses mounted. The major market indexes were sinking bow first. Eventually, the financial crisis began to eat away at consumer spending and confidence in Wall Street. The crisis spread around the globe like a slow-moving virus.

Among the hardest-hit areas were funds that specialize in financial services stocks, which were down about 47% in 2008. The collapse was devastating. Had investors been holding blue chips, they would have been better off, because financial stocks contributed in a huge way to the market decline. Many people didn't see this coming—it was well known that housing was a bubble, but could the average American have predicted how spectacular the popping of it would be? The financial sector's weighting in the S&P 500 peaked at 22.3% in 2006. As of January 2009, it was a significantly smaller 11.6%.

So how could you have protected yourself? The nice thing about trend following is that you don't have to see anything coming. The strategy is all about having you in for potential long-term upswings, but getting you out in an effort to protect you from extended losses. Investors who owned banks through the market declines and followed a disciplined plan would have avoided big losses. They also would have avoided the pain of hearing about Merrill Lynch CEO John Thain and his gilded commode.

Sector-Specific ETFs

Sector ETFs take it a step further than domestic market ETFs that track broad indexes. By targeting specific sectors, these ETFs enable you to invest in a bunch of companies in one industry instead of going out on a limb and buying an individual stock that might or might not go belly-up.

These ETFs epitomize diversity and have become more relevant as the importance of diversity becomes more apparent. Think about it: Hundreds of thousands of companies out there make up any given sector today. How can anyone pick just one to bet on? Why not hold 50 or 100 of them instead, and just target the industry overall? Finding the next Google (GOOG) or Microsoft (MSFT) is a one-in-a-million shot.

ETFs seem to be getting more specialized by the day, especially as the broad sectors have been pretty well covered. How narrow to get is entirely up to you. A broad choice, for example, is a general health-care ETF. To go narrower, other ETFs target biotechnology or pharmaceuticals.

If you want to target the transportation industry, there's an ETF for that. But if you'd rather get exposure to just airlines and subtract trucking and rail from your exposure, there's an airline ETF available to do so. You'll find broad financial ETFs, but there are regional banking and global banking funds as well. You can also find broad alternative-energy ETFs, along with solar, wind, and nuclear power funds, too.

Sector ETFs aren't simply for investors who have trouble making decisions—often you make an investment in what you believe in, and your outlook on the world comes into play. If you're invested in a healthcare ETF, perhaps you believe that the aging baby boom population will need increased medical care, raising the value of healthcare–related stocks. Perhaps you're even part of the baby boom generation and this sector has particular meaning for you.

Narrowing sector exposure to specific segments of a sector can increase volatility. Just as having a broad range of stocks within a fund can keep risk and volatility lower, so can broader exposure in a sector. But having the option to access a specific segment of a sector can also give investors the chance to identify more uptrends. For example, healthcare ETFs could be ailing, but biotechnology might be showing real mobility.

Many sectors are available in the United States and globally. Let's consider some of them.

Power Up with Utility ETFs

Utilities are also attractive because of the tax rules on the income generated by dividends paid by utilities ETFs. In a nutshell, this income is deemed qualified dividend income and is taxed at the beneficial rate of 15%, not at ordinary income rates.

So if you want to play the utilities game, you can choose from a vast array of ETFs. Here are three of them:

- **Utilities Select SPDR (XLU)** (www.spdrs.com)—The largest utility ETF. Tracks utility stocks in the S&P 500.

- **Vanguard Utilities ETF (VPU)** (www.vanguard.com)— Follows the MSCI U.S. Investable Market Utilities Index.

- **Rydex S&P Equal Weight Utilities ETF (RYU)*** (www. rydex.com)—Tracks utility stocks in the S&P 500, but weighs them all equally and is not based on market capitalization.

---

*Full disclosure: Tom Lydon is a board member of Security Global Investors/Rydex Investments.

Checking Up on Healthcare ETFs

Healthcare stocks are typically viewed as a defensive play. This sector is another area investors are eyeing toward in hopes that our healthcare system will finally see some serious reform.

Investors must watch the trend lines before jumping into any stock or ETF, and must enter with a solid strategy they can stick to. Let's take a look at a few healthcare ETFs and note their differences, because they all have something different to offer:

- **iShares Dow Jones U.S. Health Care (IYH)**—Gives exposure to 139 stocks in the healthcare sector, chosen based on market share or size. The average market cap of selected stocks is $2 billion. The expense ratio is 0.48%. (www.ishares.com)

- **Health Care Select Sector SPDR (XLV)**—Represents healthcare stocks found within the S&P 500. This is the largest ETF in the sector; it focuses on companies involved in healthcare equipment and supplies, healthcare providers and services, biotechnology, and pharmaceuticals makers. XLV's annual expenses are 0.21%.

- **Rydex S&P Equal Weight Health Care ETF (RYH)**— Follows the health-related stocks within the S&P, but stocks are weighted equally instead of by market cap. The lean is toward small to midsize companies. The index is rebalanced every quarter. RYH's annual expense ratio is 0.50%.

Banking on Financials

Although this sector has a big black eye after the events of 2008, that doesn't mean it's not a popular consideration for investment. The most popular financial ETF is the Select Sector SPDR Financial (XLF), which consists of stocks of more than 80 of the largest financial institutions in the United States. It's also one of the most heavily traded from day to day.

As with other sectors, investors have the opportunity to take very broad to very narrow views of financials. Among the other ETFs that represent this segment of the market are these:

- **KBW Regional Banking (KRE)**—Made up of 50 regional banks from around the United States. Regional banking is one of the best examples of a sector that has outperformed its parent sector, at least in 2008. Most regional banks had little to no exposure to toxic assets during the market downturn, enabling them to stay relatively healthy while their larger brethren were collapsing. It should be noted, though, that this subsector was still down—just not as sharply. (www.spdrs.com)

- **iShares Dow Jones U.S. Financial Services (IYG)**— Consists of 127 companies in the financial services sector.

- **iShares S&P Global Financials (IXG)**—Holds the stock of more than 200 financial institutions from around the world, including the United States.

- **Rydex S&P Equal Weight Financials (RYF)***—Holds more than 80 equally weighted stocks from various financial institutions.

So many sectors and subsectors exist that this should give you a good illustration of the available choices. It should also help you understand that whereas one sector might be suffering in general, you can still find investment opportunities.

---

*Full disclosure: Tom Lydon is a board member of Security Global Investors/Rydex Investments.

chapter 10

The Luster of Gold and Crude

In the late 1990s, when people jumped into technology stocks, one of the most valued and safest investments for investors—gold—got no respect. In fact, by June 1999, the world's central banks were dumping gold as fast as they could, heeding the advice of a noteworthy economist who called the yellow metal a "barbaric relic." This unloading from banks brought the price of gold to a low of $252.90 per ounce on June 21, 1999. It reflected the worst gold market in almost 30 years.

That depression didn't last long, though. Driven back up by the aftermath of the September 11 terror attacks, the "war on terror," and volatile equity markets since the collapse of the dotcom boom in 2000, the price of gold has been rising strongly since 2001. It hit an all-time high above $1,000 in March 2008.

WHAT'S THE APPEAL OF GOLD?

Why do investors go to gold? How did it become the go-to commodity in times of crisis? Gold does have applications in the industrial sector, and the obvious use of gold is in jewelry. But these safe-haven investors aren't looking to put gold to use in wiring or necklaces.

Many investors still seem to associate gold with money. Throughout history, gold has equaled money all around the world. Other metals have had varying degrees of value, but gold has always been viewed as the most valuable. From 1946 until 1971, the gold standard fixed the price of the metal at $35 per troy ounce. The system ended in 1971 when the United States stopped the direct convertibility of the dollar to gold.

Today investors purchase gold for two reasons: to gain financially from rising prices, and as a safe haven against any number of crises, ranging from economic to social. Gold is known for holding its value and helping investors preserve their assets in times of high volatility. Natalie Dempster, investment research manager at the World Gold Council (WGC), points to the metal's traditional "safe haven" characteristics as reasserting themselves in today's turbulent times. "Recently, demand has been mainly related to the financial crisis, with people looking to 'real assets' rather than paper ones," she says.

While domestic and international markets tumbled day after day in the first three months of 2008, gold climbed to a then-historic high of $1,002 an ounce. When all else looks risky, gold flourishes.

The yellow metal run that culminated in the March 2008 high began in 1999. During that time, it rose from a January 2000 level of $292 to a high of $1002.80 in March 2008, for an increase of nearly 243%, shown in Figure 10.1.

The run-up of gold prices in this time period provided investors with vast opportunities to capture an uptrend. Despite the beginnings of a recession taking hold in December 2007, there were still opportunities to be had in the markets. Although gold is a volatile metal and is particularly subject to the whims of the markets and the fears of investors, having an entry-and-exit strategy enables investors to capture some momentum.

Money manager Rick Holbrook was in commodities, oil stocks, and natural resources during the bull years of 2003–2007. He attempted to capture the uptrends by minding the trend lines. "You can never guess when it's going to drop or when it's going to bottom," he says. "Rather than try to guess myself...in most markets, I try to understand what the message is."

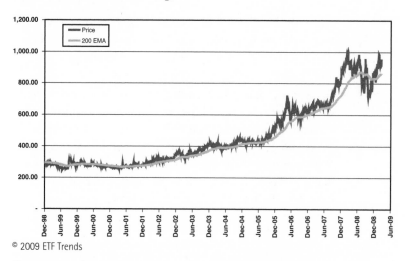

© 2009 ETF Trends

Figure 10.1   *Gold with 200-day moving average, 1998–2009*

A HISTORICAL PEEK AT WHAT MAKES GOLD TICK

Investors tend to flock to gold as a safe harbor in troubled times. Three other influential factors can lead to a run-up in the price of gold:

- **A weak dollar typically boosts gold prices.** For example, a look back in history shows that when the dollar fell in 1982 and 1983, the price of gold rose from $294 an ounce to $514 an ounce in just nine months—an increase of 74%. This happened again from 1985 to 1987, when a drop in the dollar propelled the price of gold from $282 to $502 over 21 months—an increase of 78%.

- Gold has also flourished in times of high inflation. Since the end of World War II, the five steepest years of U.S. inflation were 1946, 1974, 1975, 1979, and 1980. During those five years, the average real return on stocks, as measured by the Dow, was −12.33%; the average real return on gold was 130.4%. During the 1970s, gold soared to 23 times its value.

- Historically, gold has been highly correlated to the price of oil. The price of gold has experienced two major upward moves since 1968. The first occurred between 1972 and 1974, when oil prices climbed 325%. During the same period, gold prices rose 268% (on a quarterly average basis). The second major price move occurred between 1978 and 1980, when oil prices increased 105%. Over the same period, quarterly average gold prices rose 254%.

Oil: A Slippery, Yet Profitable Slope

Why would someone invest in oil? As one of the most important natural resources known to man, it's known as "black gold" for good reason. Many economies are fueled by oil (no pun intended), and oil has made many people very, very rich. And as a finite natural resource, oil is only increasing in value as concerns swirl about how much of it is left.

Nearly everything we do is somehow driven by oil. It's used to heat our homes, run our cars, create plastics, and more. The companies involved in the production of oil these days are reaping record corporate profits. As democracy and capitalism flourish around the world, so does oil demand.

No wonder investors want a piece of this. Oil might be dirtier than gold, but it's an asset that tends to rise in price during inflationary periods and in times of high demand. To be sitting on oil is to be sitting on high potential for reward, because as hard as we might try, eliminating the need for oil is proving to be a challenging task. But as always, the more rewarding something can be, the more risky it is, too.

Oil can be a tough commodity to invest in because so many factors affect its price—and very quickly. Among them are

- **Weather**—Hurricanes, tornadoes, and other catastrophic events can wreck drilling stations, interrupting production.
- **Politics**—Bombings, wars, fires, and so on can destroy pipelines, disrupting supply.
- **Oil-producing countries**—Countries that produce the most oil wield the most power when it comes to pricing and supplies. We're at the mercy of these regions because they have a hand in artificially setting prices. This makes it difficult for investors to play oil, because the price might not always translate into what the price should actually be.

Investments in oil can be extremely lucrative or give you a serious case of heartburn. Oil is no doubt one of the most volatile commodities in the universe, subject to the whims of demand, the weather, and political tensions.

Although oil is incredibly volatile, as you can see in Figure 10.2, trend following can help protect you from excessively heavy losses if you hit the escape button at the right time. After the 2002 bear market, oil prices went on a rebound. Markets grew and recovered, demand increased accordingly, and before anyone knew it, oil had surpassed levels beyond anyone's imagination.

The crux of the run-up in 2008, though, was that global demand vastly outstripped global supply. Countries such as China and India are thirsty for oil to fuel their economic growth, yet the world's oil-producing regions are producing less oil, to keep prices beyond anyone's reach (except maybe Yao Ming's). According to the IEA, oil demand will advance by an annual average of 1.6% between 2006 and 2030, from an approximate current level of 86 million barrels to 106 million barrels in 2030. In other words, daily demand in 2030 will be 23% higher.

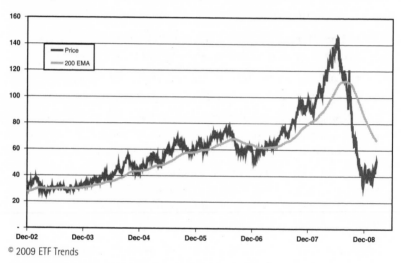

© 2009 ETF Trends

Figure 10.2 *Oil prices with 200-day moving average, 2002–2008*

Until 2006, the average investor was unable to capture this stunning growth with any amount of ease. Futures contracts are tricky (and expensive) investing tools that need to be "rolled over" to avoid taking physical possession of the commodity. In April 2006, an ETF launched that invested in oil futures, so all investors had to do was buy the fund, the United States Oil (USO) (www.unitedstatesoilfund. com). The ETF handles the contract rollover.

During the bull period for oil prices, billions flew into USO. This has led many on Wall Street to believe that the popularity of USO has further contributed to the run-up in oil prices that ended in July 2008 at $147.27 a barrel.

Oil fell from that high point in 2008 to less than $50 a barrel by early 2009, as the global recession hit its stride. Demand decreased, the gross domestic product (GDP) in the United States went negative, and people stopped driving and spending. Oil lost around 70% of its value during that time period. If you had bought USO at the buy signal and exited as cracks began to show in the price of oil, you would have managed to protect some very significant profits. If you had hung on even as oil declined in the hopes that it would once again regain its momentum, you lost a good chunk of change.

Turning Trends into Profits

Where will oil go from here? Demand looks to be growing and supply could be dwindling. Still, no one knows for sure what direction oil is headed. In fact, no one ever knows for sure where any investment will head: not Japan markets, not technology, not emerging markets, not gold, not even domestic markets. Unfortunately, it's easy to get hung up on fundamentals. We love to make predictions—it's in our blood.

Investor Ted Spickler admitted his own tendency to get hung up on what's expected to happen down the line. He owns an energy fund that has fallen well off its highs, and he logically knows he should let it go. But reports about the future direction of oil have him hanging on.

Let the position go if the trend isn't there. It doesn't matter what the fundamentals say. If it's meant to be, the trend will come back and you can buy back in. Remember the hokey greeting card saying, "If you love something, set it free"? It actually applies here. Making predictions is a disaster waiting to happen—don't do it. Forget about using your gut feelings, and just say "no" to your well-intentioned neighbors and best friends when it comes to both drugs and stock tips. The best way to determine the beginning and end to any trend—and, therefore, enhance your odds of profiting—is to monitor a sector's 200-day moving average and let the numbers speak for themselves.

As has become evident in recent months, investors love to talk about gold and oil. Many of them feel a sense of satisfaction in being able to describe and predict based on the current economic environment. But in reality, as in any market, it's difficult to make these predictions. Gold and oil represent their own asset classes and have shown to be incredibly volatile. It makes sense, instead, to have a specific strategy when investing in these areas: during many ten-year periods, you would have owned these commodities and made no money.

Owning Your Share of Commodities

Historically, commodities have been viewed as a completely separate asset class. Areas such as gold and oil have become known for their volatility. But commodities rarely correlate perfectly to the world's stock markets. Because commodities operate along their own individual trends and are now available in ETF form, they can make excellent additions to any portfolio.

Today, you now have many options for participating in a commodities bull market. You can find futures, physical commodities, or baskets of stocks consisting of commodities producers. This hasn't always been the case, however. Before the influx of ETFs, you, as an individual investor, were simply left out in the cold. For decades, commodities remained the exclusive domain of professional traders, large companies, and hedge funds—and for good reason.

Futures trading requires an in-depth understanding of economic trends, the ability to anticipate the impact those trends will have on the cost of goods, and the willingness to monitor trading activity on a daily basis. It's not for the faint-of-heart. Risk and reward are high, but before commodities ETFs, you had to know the game intimately. Owning physical commodities isn't exactly feasible unless you have an airplane hangar at your disposal.

Now, though, you have the most simple and diversified tool at your disposal to access commodities. Investor Ron Exner says, "I use ETFs as a way to participate in the commodities market without the risk of contract ownership." Through his strategy, he says, he continues to generate income from what would otherwise be "a relatively static, nonincome-bearing investment." Exner prefers ETFs when it comes to investing. "I like using ETFs because of their low fees and the fact that they move counter to the weakening dollar and slouching U.S. economy," he says.

Commodity ETFs come in various shapes and sizes. Chances are, you can find a fund type that's a natural fit for your portfolio:

- **Physical commodities**—The most direct way to own a commodity is to actually buy the commodity. But the hassle of buying, storing, and selling gold is not very practical. Instead, you can buy an ETF that buys gold, and your shares give you partial ownership of the physical metal.

- **Individual commodity futures**—The main factor determining the performance of an ETF linked to commodity futures is changes in the spot price of the underlying commodity. The spot price is the current price of the commodity; as it changes, so does the value of the future contracts based on it. If the spot price goes up, the value of the futures contracts goes up, and so does the value of a share of an ETF holding these futures. One aspect to keep in mind with respect to this type of ETF is that any gains or losses generated throughout the year within the fund are taxed as 60% long-term and 40% short-term gains, regardless of how long the contracts were held. At current rates, this works out to a maximum 23% capital gains rate—higher than for stocks, but lower than for collectibles.

- **Commodity indexes**—ETFs linked to commodity indexes enable investors to diversify their holdings. For example, you can invest in a broad-based ETF to give you plays on individual commodities such as soybeans, corn, sugar, and wheat; or you can buy an ETF that gives you pieces of agriculture, energy, and metals.

- **Commodity equities**—Finally, ETFs linked to commodity equities hold a basket of companies that make or process a commodity. These have a different risk/return profile than commodities futures alone. They expose the investor to company risk in addition to issues related to the specific commodity. This can be good or bad. Investors have the additional upside of appreciation in individual company stocks, but prices of company stock also can go down in response to company-specific events.

How you choose to get your exposure to commodities depends on how you want to access them and what you're comfortable with. As we get into the various commodity ETFs available today, you'll see that you have vast choices. Furthermore, you can decide how focused you want to get. Sector ETFs can be broad or narrow, and so can commodity ETFs.

Agriculture

Costs for energy and land, the two biggest factors affecting agricultural pricing, have risen sharply in the past several years. By 2020, the world will have an expected 3 billion additional people. This means we'll essentially have to figure out how to double global agriculture production over the next 13 years just to meet the population growth of the world. Commodities in this category include both raw and processed goods. Some of the agricultural commodities most in demand are corn, soybeans, wheat, coffee, cocoa, sugar, cotton, cattle, and hogs.

Consider the following ETFs for a taste of agriculture:

- **PowerShares DB Agriculture (DBA)** (www.invesco powershares.com)—Tracks the Deutsche Bank Liquid Commodity Index—Optimum Yield Agriculture Excess Return. It contains futures contracts on corn, soybeans, wheat, and sugar.

- **Market Vectors Global Agribusiness (MOO)** (www. vaneck.com)—Tracks the DAXglobal Agribusiness Index. Its top components include Mosaic Co. (MOS), Potash Corp. (POT), Monsanto Corp. (MON), Deere & Co. (DE), and Archer-Daniels-Midland (ADM).

Energy

Energy commodities not only fuel the growth of world economies, but they also directly affect our daily lives via increased gas, heating, and electrical prices. Because the demand for energy resources is expected to continue to grow as supplies of traditional fuels dwindle, costs will likely climb further.

As China, India, and other emerging economies continue to build thousands of factories, and as their massive populations become more affluent consumers, energy demands will increase exponentially. In today's world, energy mainly comes from oil and gas, both natural resources that have a finite supply. The supply of oil—and, thus, its price—is affected by a number of events. Among them are world unrest, the political climate, and weather events such as hurricanes, to name just a few.

Before you decide to get into the energy sector, it's especially wise to watch the trends. Not only can unprecedented events send it spinning out of control, but this area of commodities seems more ripe than most for idle speculation. You can easily become swept up in a frenzy.

- **United States Oil Fund (USO)**—Tracks the price of West Texas Intermediate light, sweet crude oil using futures contracts.

- **PowerShares DB Energy Fund (DBE)**—Tracks the Deutsche Bank Liquid Commodity Index—Optimum Yield Energy Excess Return. It tracks the prices of crude oil, heating oil, gasoline, and natural gas.

- **United States Gasoline (UGA)**—Tracks the price of gasoline using futures contracts. (www.unitedstatesgasolinefund. com)

- **iShares Dow Jones U.S. Energy Sector Index Fund (IYE)**—Tracks the Dow Jones U.S. Oil & Gas Index. Its top holdings include Chevron (CVX), ConocoPhillips (COP), Exxon Mobil (XOM), and Transocean (RIG). (www.ishares. com)

Metals (Precious, Base, and Industrial)

Metals include copper, gold, platinum, palladium, silver, and steel. They are used for industrial purposes, in construction, and for jewelry. Geopolitical and economic factors in the dominant producing (South Africa, the United States, and Australia) and consuming (India and the United States) countries affect the price action for metals, but each type also has its own unique fundamental influences.

- **SPDR Gold Shares Fund (GLD) and iShares COMEX Gold Trust (IAU)** (www.spdrs.com; www.ishares.com)—Both hold physical gold bullion.

- **PowerShares DB Gold Fund (DGL)**—Tracks the Deutsche Bank Liquid Commodity Index. It tracks the price of gold using futures contracts.

- **Market Vectors Steel (SLX)**—Tracks the AMEX Steel Index. Its top holdings include Rio Tinto (RTP), Arcelor Mittal (**MT.AS**), and Companhia Vale ADS (RIO).

- **iShares Silver Trust (SLV)**—Holds physical silver.

- **PowerShares DB Base Metals (DBB)**—Tracks the Deutsche Bank Liquid Commodity Index—Optimum Yield Industrial Metals Excess Return. Its holdings consist of futures contracts on aluminum, zinc, and copper (grade A).

Broad-Based Commodity ETFs

If you're finding it a challenge deciding which commodity segment will do best in the long term, you might find it easier to just go broad and track the overall sector.

- **iShares S&P GSCI Commodity Indexed Trust (GSG)**—Tracks the GSCI Excess Return index. Its holdings consist of futures contracts on 24 commodities, including energy, agriculture, and precious metals.

- **PowerShares DB Commodity Index Tracking Fund (DBC)**—Tracks the Deutsche Bank Liquid Commodity Index. Its holdings consist of futures contracts on commodities such as energy, gold, corn, and aluminum.

Going the Roundabout Way

If you find yourself having trouble deciding whether you would prefer commodity or single-country exposure in your portfolio, you can have it both ways and kill two birds with one stone by looking into ETFs of countries rich with commodities and natural resources. Many global markets are dependent on their commodities markets; they are a large part of their economies.

But why should you consider single-country funds? These funds allow for some commodity exposure and provide more diversity over picking a single-commodity fund. You should note that some funds are heavily weighted in commodities and their economies could be *too* dependent on them—Russia's energy dependence is a prime example. It is worth the few extra minutes to peruse the finer details of specific country funds.

Although there are many different commodity-rich countries to choose from, the following are just some examples of countries that are rich in commodities.

South Africa

This country's miners are the largest producers of platinum, gold, and chromium. South Africa is an emerging market with a large middle class. They have natural resources and developed financial, legal, communications, energy, and transport sectors. But the high level of joblessness and poor infrastructure does constrain growth. The government tries to control inflation, have budget surpluses, and create jobs through government-owned enterprises.

iShares MSCI South Africa Index (EZA)
(www.ishares.com)
Materials make up nearly 30% of the fund.

Chile

Chile's economy favors foreign trade and has healthy financial institutions. Commodities make up around 75% of total exports, and exports are 40% of GDP. Copper is a main staple of the country, which accounts for 33% of government revenue. The government adheres to a counter-cyclical fiscal policy by holding wealth from trade surpluses during economic growth, and goes into deficit spending when their growth is low or copper prices are down.

iShares MSCI Chile Investable Mkt Idx (ECH)
Materials make up nearly 20% of the fund.

Russia

Since 2000, Russia has improved its financial sector and has had high trade surpluses. But the positive trends started to reverse in the second half of 2008. Their banks are now faced with liquidity problems. The economy is heavily reliant on energy and raw materials. Investors are wary of the country's corruption, institutions, and exchange rates.

Market Vectors Russia ETF (RSX) (www.vaneck.com)
Energy makes up 40% of the fund.

Australia

This is the world's largest net exporter of coal. Australia has a high per capita GDP. The government focuses on reforms, low inflation, housing market, and ties with trading partners like China. In recent years, their exporters of raw materials and agricultural products enjoyed the high prices of commodities. The government may also provide a fiscal stimulus to deter slow growth in 2009.

iShares MSCI Australia Index (EWA)
Materials make up 25% of the fund.

Commodities: A Valuable Part of Your Portfolio

The greatest benefit of adding commodities to your portfolio is that, as the value of commodities rises and falls in response to the same economic, social, political, or environmental forces that affect stocks, commodities tend to move in the opposite direction.

Plus, unlike stocks, which can lose value and even be removed from trading for nonperformance, leaving investors to take a loss, commodities always will have some value to us and our lives, although that value will continue to fluctuate with global economic growth.

chapter 11

The World of Currencies

A dollar doesn't get what it used to these days. For decades, citizens of the United States who went abroad could eat the finest meals and stay in luxury accommodations, largely on the strength of the U.S. dollar. But those days seem to be over. In recent years, the dollar has become significantly weaker than other major currencies. At one point, US$1 was worth half of £1. After the euro came into being, the weak dollar made traveling to European countries that used the currency an expensive proposition.

But having a strong or weak currency is never uniformly a good or bad thing. You should consider the implications for both circumstances. Imports and exports can suffer when two currencies have vastly different values. With a weak dollar, you may be less inclined to purchase luxury goods manufactured in countries with much stronger currencies. Meanwhile, manufacturers in countries with stronger currencies worry because their U.S. sales are down.

Monitoring the Ups and Downs of Money

The foreign exchange market (or *forex*, as it's known) involves a lot of moving parts, especially when it comes to investing in the money supply of all global economies. It's much larger than the typical stock exchange and every bit as challenging to attempt to predict. Just as no one knows where the stock market or commodity prices are ultimately going, no one knows where currencies are going on a day-to-day basis, either. No one has come up with a foolproof method of charting the future on a daily basis. And those who think they know how to do it are usually wrong. For this reason, currencies have a place in an overall trend following strategy.

Although highly volatile, following the trends of any given currency can help keep risk low and reward high. Let's start by talking about the one we know most about: the U.S. dollar.

A Rocky Road for the U.S. Dollar

Unfortunately, when you look at the U.S. dollar's relative value over the past 40 years, it's been a bumpy, pothole-filled road.

Outside of a temporary uptrend in the dollar in 1997–2001, currencies from Germany, Switzerland, Japan, Europe, and Canada all out-valued the U.S. dollar. After that short run, the dollar petered out, tumbling 42% versus the euro and 20% against the Canadian dollar and others from 2001 to 2008. As noted in the Grandfather Foreign Exchange Report, "For every $100,000 of a citizen's assets, the international buying power dropped $42,000 since 2001 versus the euro."

Citizens Suffer

Starting in 1997, Treasury officials began voicing support for a strong dollar with the hope of reducing trade balances. Primarily a public relations ploy, it provided only a brief recovery for the dollar.

The dollar's slight uptick in 1997–2001 occurred despite all-time-high trade deficits each year and soaring ratios of private-sector debt in consumer, business, and financial sectors. This encouraged overconsumption of imports instead of American-made goods and services.

From 2001–2008, many U.S. citizens felt the effects of a weakening dollar through their stock market assets. Those assets lost value as the purchasing power of the greenback eroded with huge market declines and an economy devastated by soaring debt. In simple terms, not only have those assets declined relative to others here in the United States, but citizens outside the United States could buy those assets less expensively, because their currency has appreciated compared to the U.S. dollar.

The most conservative, who stayed away from the market to protect their savings, at least came out with their assets intact but were later horrified to witness interest earnings on their assets chopped more than 80% during 2001–2008. You may recall that's when the Federal Reserve forced interest rates to record-low levels. On top of this came the huge depreciation of all dollar assets in terms of its international value, as the dollar dramatically fell.

Here's what went on during that period (and others) to weaken the dollar's value. Some say the government caused this situation, believing that a weak dollar would turn trade deficits into surpluses by boosting exports. Instead, negative trade balances exploded as the U.S. manufacturing base faltered.

More recent causes for the dollar's bearish condition include a softening U.S. labor market, deepening turmoil in housing, and 2007 growth slowing to the worst pace in five years. And in 2008–2009, the Federal Reserve flooded the market with billions of dollars, further threatening to weaken the currency.

In addition, high oil prices are driving up the already above-trend U.S. trade deficit, flooding the world with more dollars. Finally, the United States continues to import more than it exports, increasing U.S. demand for foreign currencies and further reducing the dollar's value dramatically against the euro, as shown in Figure 11.1.

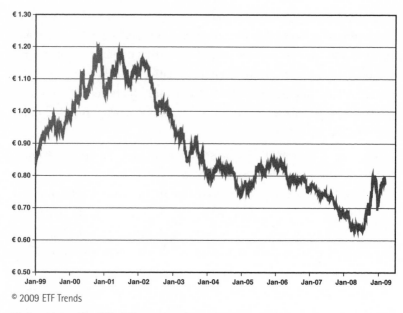

© 2009 ETF Trends

Figure 11.1   *The U.S. dollar versus the euro, 1999–2009*

The Dollar Bucks Its Trend—Will It Last?

Just as I've talked about following the trends in other sectors, currencies go through up-and-down trends and can be followed using a 200-day moving average. Currencies can enhance portfolio returns and lower volatility, are independent of stock and bond prices, and can be a way to diversify risk and introduce new sources of return.

As long as the U.S. dollar remains weak, trends tend to favor foreign currencies. Instead of predicting when the dollar will rebound, you can wait for the euro or Swiss franc to go below their trend lines. Although the U.S. dollar finally busted through a long-term downtrend in mid-2008, breaking above its 200-day moving average, many people believe that the dollar will continue its decline against other currencies around the world. Trend followers, of course, let the numbers speak for themselves.

HOW CURRENCIES ARE VALUED

How are the values of these currencies determined? A number of factors come into play:

- **Political conditions**—How stable is the government? Is it corrupt? Can it be bribed? Does the country play well with others, especially big players such as the United States, China, and Russia? Take a look at the form of government: Is it a dictatorship? Communist? A democracy?

- **The economy**—The unemployment rate, the country's overall work ethic, inflation, and the general direction of the economy are all factors. Also, is the country older or newer? What is its chief industry (technology, agriculture, manufacturing)? Does the government run a budget/trade surplus or deficit? Does it have to borrow heavily? Are interest rates going up or down within their monetary system (up is bullish for the currency)?

- **Outside perception**—Appearances shouldn't matter, but like it or not, they do. Perception might have no basis in reality, but news reports, movies, newspapers, and good old-fashioned rumors can affect how a country appears to the rest of the world. Another factor in a currency's value is how much is known about its country. The less is known, the lower the value. This is one instance when it doesn't pay to be an enigma.

- **Demographics**—A young population tends to signal a bright future full of people who are open to growth, new ideas, and change.

- **Public figures**—Whether leading the country or merely being famous, the best-known people in a country can hold great sway over how their homeland is perceived.

- **Level of openness**—Privacy costs a country's currency. Cuba has been isolated for some time. China is becoming more open. Venezuela is becoming more isolated. If a country is slowly becoming closed off from the outside world, its currency will suffer.

- **Natural resources**—How in-demand is a country's resources? If value is perceived (whether legitimately or not), the currency will go up.

- **Weather**—Not only is the type of weather and the severity of it important, but how a country responds to weather-related disasters is a factor in its currency value. All this affects how the outside world perceives the country, and it will be a less attractive tourist destination if its response to disaster is poor.

- **War and conflicts**—Who are the country's allies? Who are its enemies? How strong is the military? Is the country at war or experiencing civil conflict, border disputes, internal genocide, or other problems?

- **Education**—The level of education of a country's population affects the value of the currency. How connected are they to the Internet? Do they speak a number of languages? Does the country have a lot of scientists, inventors, and authors?

Making the Most Out of Currency ETFs

Currency ETFs have simplified investment in this market for millions of people. In 2007, the forex market garnered $3.2 trillion dollars worth of transactions each day. This makes the market the quiet giant of finance, towering over all other capital markets in its world.

But there are things you need to know about these ETFs, and this complex and interesting market overall. Some of the key points to currency trading are

- **When trading currencies, yield drives return.** When you trade currencies, you are actually buying and selling two underlying currencies, and all currencies are quoted in pairs because currencies are valued in relation to one another. For this reason, the yield between the two becomes important: Say Currency X has a yield of 4% and Currency Y has a yield of 1%. If you go long on X/Y, you will earn 4%, but will have to pay 1%. Your net is 3%.

- **The forex allows huge leverage.** Often as high as 100:1, which means that you can control $10,000 worth of assets with as little as $100 of capital. Remember though, leverage works both ways.

- **Since currency values never stay the same, the carry trade became a popular play on the market.** The carry trade involves selling one currency with a low interest rate and then using the proceeds to buy a different currency that yields a higher interest rate. For example, an investor borrows 1,000 yen and converts the money into U.S. dollars and buys a bond for an equivalent amount. Assuming the bond pays 5% and the Japanese interest rate is 0%, the trader stands to make a profit of 5% if the interest rates between Japan and the United States don't change. The interest rates are the risk in the carry trade, as well: If the dollar loses value to the yen, money is lost.

- **Interest rates matter—a lot.** Becoming familiar with the economics and currency of the country in which you are trading will help you understand when inflation is looming and when opportunity is knocking.

When entering the currency market, there are eight major currencies worth trading, which give you the best over- or under-valued opportunities. The eight countries that make up the largest portion of the currency trading market are the United States, the Eurozone (Germany, France, Italy, and Spain), Japan, United Kingdom, Switzerland, Australia, Canada, and New Zealand. There are many more than this, though.

Security Global Investors/Rydex Investments offers eight currency-focused ETFs—the first such ETFs—called CurrencyShares (www.currencyshares.com). They're structured as grantor trusts that hold the underlying currency, and they gain or lose value based on exchange rates and any overnight interest accrued. Grantor trusts relate to the taxation of a trust's income—in this case, the grantor pays the tax (in other situations, the trust and/or its beneficiaries would pay it).

The CurrencyShares Fund includes these ETFs:

- **CurrencyShares Japanese Yen (FXY)**
- **CurrencyShares Euro (FXE)**
- **CurrencyShares Swedish Krona (FXS)**

Instead of picking a direction for any one currency, and to get the most diversification, you might consider the **PowerShares DB G10 Currency Harvest (DBV)**, launched by PowerShares in September 2006. It trades on the view that, historically, currencies with higher interest rates outperform those with lower rates. (The G10 is a group of the ten major industrialized countries—Belgium, Canada, France, Germany, Italy, Japan, the Netherlands, Sweden, Britain, and the United States.)

Essentially, the ETF incorporates a carry trade by going long on the futures of the three currencies with the highest interest rates and going short on those with the lowest rates. Those rates are reviewed every quarter, and the longs and shorts are reallocated, if necessary. The fund seeks to track the Deutsche Bank G10 Currency Future Harvest Index.

WisdomTree (www.wisdomtree.com) also has a line of currency ETFs that seek to earn current income reflective of money market rates available to U.S. investors. These funds include the following:

- **WisdomTree Dreyfus Chinese Yuan Fund (CYB)**
- **WisdomTree Dreyfus Indian Rupee Fund (ICN)**
- **WisdomTree Dreyfus Brazilian Real Fund (BZF)**

In May 2009, WisdomTree also launched the **WisdomTree Dreyfus Emerging Currency Fund (CEW)**, a basket of 11 emerging market currencies, giving exposure through the use of forward contracts.

There are also two ways to play the movements of the U.S. dollar directly: **PowerShares DB U.S. Dollar Bullish (UUP),** and **PowerShares DB U.S. Dollar Bearish (UDN)**. If the dollar looks weak, UDN is one way to try to capitalize. On the other hand, as the dollar gains steam, UUP might be an option if a clear uptrend emerges.

Squeezing the Most from Your Dollars

Currency ETFs have grown especially popular in the time since the first such fund was launched. Aside from the diversification they offer, investors enjoy taking advantage of international interest-rate adjustments and geopolitical issues.

The main advantage of trading with a currency ETF is the same advantage offered to other ETFs: transparency. The exchange rate is listed and everyone gets the same price, unlike when you attempt to buy currency in a foreign country and get a little ripped off. Because there's a minimum trade of one share, the investment an investor has to make is much smaller than in a typical foreign exchange trade.

Worldwide currency can be volatile and is affected by a wide range of factors. Currency ETFs give you a way to bet against the U.S. dollar and gain foreign market exposure without betting and possibly losing the entire farm. If you feel that you're ready to get involved, here's what you should know:

- Currency ETFs have different tax rules than regular ETFs. Interest income and gains are taxed at the ordinary income tax rate instead of at the long-term capital gains rate.

- Read the newspaper. Check out the political situation of the country's currency you've invested in. Some areas are more volatile than others, but you should always be paying attention to the factors that could determine whether the currency rises or falls.

- Don't put all your eggs in one basket. ETFs can be a simple way to get exposure to a basket of several currencies, thereby spreading around the risk.

- Patience is key. Don't dive in and out of currency ETFs hoping to score big. Know how much risk is involved.

- Keep in mind that many IRA-qualified accounts don't typically permit currency trading, and institutions often are restricted from holding certain assets but are permitted to hold ETFs. Voilá—the currency ETF solves that problem, and everyone wins while still following the rules.

chapter 12

Trends in Fixed Income*

It can be easy to forget about bonds, especially during the good times in the market. Often, this is a segment of the market that investors might tend to dismiss as something for "conservative" investors who are nearing retirement. But recently, the bond market has been getting far more attention as allocations shift from equities and from alternative investments. Indeed, from a risk/return basis, many parts of the bond market look very appealing compared to almost any asset class.

Whether that's true or not, bonds do have one thing in common with the rest of the market: They have their own trends. Bonds also range on a scale from "very safe" to "very aggressive" (and risky). Risk in bonds comes in a few different flavors, including traditional return volatility as measured by standard deviation. However, bonds also have interest rate risk, which is their sensitivity to changing rates. Longer maturity bonds will be more sensitive to interest rate changes while short-term funds will have less sensitivity. Knowing this, an investor can determine the risk parameters they might want to accept in a fund and position it appropriately in an asset allocation.

*Chip Norton, who contributed substantially to this chapter, is the managing director of Fixed Income Strategies at Naples, Florida–based Wasmer, Schroeder & Company. Chip has specialized in the fixed income markets for more than 25 years and is author of *Investing for Income* (1999, McGraw Hill).

The different types of bonds, from safest to most risky, are as follows:

- **U.S. Treasury bonds**—These bonds are considered among the safest because the government of any stable country rarely defaults on its debt. In exchange for safety, yields (the interest or dividends received) are generally low. The yields on Treasury bonds hit 50-year lows in 2008 as investors sought safety from the markets. In fact, at one point, yields went negative—meaning people were paying the government to hold their money.

- **Municipal bonds**—These bonds are issued by states and localities. Although they're not as safe as Treasuries, they do offer a measure of safety. It's unusual for cities and states to go bankrupt because they can usually raise revenue through taxes—but bankruptcies do happen. A bonus of these bonds is that they're free from federal taxes.

- **Corporate bonds**—These bonds reside on the higher end of the risk spectrum, because corporations can—and do—default on their debt. Because of their higher risk, they come with high yields.

- **Junk bonds**—These bonds, sometimes known as *high-yield*, are the riskiest of all, rated below investment grade at the time of purchase. These types of bonds are also frequently known as *high-yield debt*. Of course, because of their extreme risk, they tend to pay the most handsome yields.

- **Foreign bonds**—You don't have to limit yourself to the United States when it comes to bonds. Foreign governments, municipalities, and corporations also issue debt, denominated in their own currencies. There are different levels of risk in these bonds, just as there are in the U.S. bond market. The principal risk with these is currency risk, which is the potential for loss because of exchange rate fluctuations.

BOND BUBBLES

Bond bubbles can and do happen. In fact, as of late 2008 to early 2009, it was believed that the markets were in a Treasury bubble. A wave of market fear sent investors scurrying to safety in Treasuries, which sent yields to historic lows. The upside, of course, was that these "safe" funds had some of the best total return of any bonds ever.

The government also issued a mountain of Treasury bonds to finance a host of bailout plans, which led many to suspect that an oversupply of the paper would eventually lead to a drop in demand. That demand drop would lead to a crash in prices, saddling investors with the losses from which they were trying to insulate themselves. However, these bubbles also present buying opportunities. Consider the bubble that burst in the junk bond market in the early 1990s. Once the bubble burst and prices declined, investors moved in to find value and rode an almost 10-year uptrend in prices with the added benefit of high yields.

HOW BONDS CAN HELP YOU

Bonds are among the most versatile and useful investment vehicles around, but their benefits might be a mystery to you. They can:

- Grow capital with high-yield returns—The higher risk bonds can be of interest if you're looking for ways to grow and sock away money. However, do your research and be aware of the risks.

- Diversification—Bonds can help you spread your risk around in your portfolio, and bonds can help stabilize or even enhance your returns.

- **Extra income**—Bonds can help you preserve your principal while at the same time generating interest income for you to spend right now.
- **Savings preservation**—If you're looking at the future and see big expenditures up ahead—college, a wedding, a house, retirement—bonds with a maturity date matching the date you'll need the money can give you an assist.

WHAT YOU NEED AND WHEN YOU NEED IT

An important thing to know about bonds is what you need and when you need it, as well as what kind of risk you can tolerate. The needs of a 20-year-old are going to be far different from those of an 80-year-old. Bonds can accommodate these age differences and work to help you realize your goals at any age:

- **In your 20s and 30s**—You are focused on making money, and your risk level tends to be high to moderate. Bonds are likely to be a smaller portion of your portfolio than they will be as you age.

- **In your 40s and 50s**—Your risk level starts to go down, and you gradually increase your exposure to safer bonds and start to transition out of riskier bond types.

- **In your 60s and beyond**—You're likely retiring, or thinking about doing it soon. At this point, you hope that you have a nice, solid portfolio with enough money to live on, and you want to protect that money. Many experts suggest that at this age, you should increase your bond allocation to at least 50%.

Factors to Consider

Bonds are tricky instruments, subject to a number of factors. There are several points investors should understand:

- As bonds increase in price, their yield tends to go down. In periods of high demand (such as market turmoil, when investors are seeking safety), the price of a Treasury bond tends to rise while the yields fall (see Figure 12.1). Prices of corporate bonds in down markets, however, tend to fall while yields increase—after all, would you be so keen to invest in a corporation's bonds in a recessionary climate?

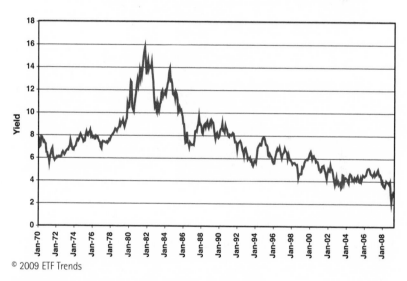

© 2009 ETF Trends

Figure 12.1   *10-year U.S. Treasury bond, 1970–2008*

- Credit quality is one of the main criteria when it comes to judging the investment quality of a bond. The rating clues investors in to a bond's "credit worthiness" or default risk. The rating is a grade given by a private, independent ratings service (such as Standard & Poor's or Moody's), which indicates their credit quality. These ratings are given to illustrate the bond issuer's strength, or in other words, their ability to pay a bond's principal plus interest in a timely manner. Credit quality does change over time and often deteriorates during recessionary periods. Indeed, prior to the market crash in 2007 and 2008, the default rates on high bonds were as low as 1.5%. The expectation today is that default rates could exceed 15% on this type of bond. Conversely, municipal credit quality has been historically low and is expected to continue to show low defaults (see Figure 12.2).

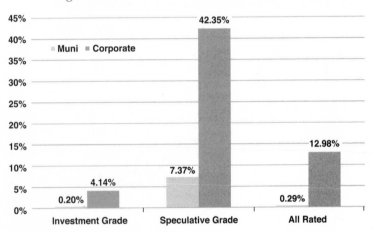

Source: Municipal Market Advisors

Figure 12.2 *Municipal market versus corporate market default credit summary, 1986–2008*

The ratings services use their own letter grades, but as an example, Standard & Poor's uses the following scale:

- **AAA and AA**—High credit quality
- **AA and BBB**—Medium credit quality
- **BB, B, CCC, CC, and C**—Low credit quality (also known as *junk bonds*)
- **D**—Bonds in default

- Yield refers to the income return on an investment and is expressed annually as a percentage. Bonds have four yields:

  - **Coupon**—The bond interest rate fixed at issuance.

  - **Current yield**—The annual return earned on the price paid for a bond.

  - **Yield to maturity**—The total return an investor receives by holding the bond to maturity. The yield reflects all the interest payments from the time of purchase to maturity, including interest on interest. It also includes any appreciation or depreciation in the bond's price.

  - **Tax equivalent**—Nontaxable municipal bonds will have a tax equivalent yield, which is determined by an investor's tax bracket.

One of the biggest risks with bonds is interest rate risk. Interest rates and bonds share an inverse relationship: As interest rates fall, prices increase, and vice versa. Why does this happen? Typically, it's because investors are trying to lock in the highest rates possible, for as long as possible. To do so, they'll get existing bonds that pay a higher rate than the prevailing market rate. This leads to an increase in demand, which means the price increases and the interest rate falls. A good rule of thumb is that bonds with shorter maturities will suffer less from an increase in interest rates. But if you're holding bonds in a period of low inflation and low yields (2008 is a perfect example), long-term bonds tend to deliver the biggest gains.

The Yield Curve

Why is the *yield curve* important? It can be a good leading indicator of economic activity, and it can indicate where investors think the economy is headed. The yield curve plots the interest rates, at a set point in time, of bonds with equal credit quality but differing maturity dates. It's primarily used to predict changes in economic output and growth.

The yield curve is a line graph that plots the relationship between yields to maturity and time to maturity for bonds of the same asset class and credit quality. The plotted line begins with the spot interest rate (the rate for the shortest maturity) and extends out in time, generally for 30 years.

This curve shows the yield differences that are due solely to maturity differences, and it shows the overall relationship that prevails at a given time in the marketplace between rates and maturities. An upward sloping yield curve means that bond yields generally rise as the maturity lengthens.

The yield curve has been known to slope down, a sign of recession, but it rarely stays that way for long. Flat curves signal a slowdown, which often happens when the Federal Reserve raises interest rates to keep the economy from growing too quickly.

If you learn to read the yield curve, it can help you structure your portfolio. For example, you can use it to identify bonds that appear cheap (or expensive) at any given time. Because the yield curve depicts yield at various maturities, one can visually see how much yield they can achieve for a specific time horizon. The curvature or "slope" of the yield curve is dynamic and reflects investor preferences at a specific point in time. For example, a *steep yield curve* means short-term rates are very low compared to low-term rates and suggests there is value in the longer-term maturities. A *flat yield curve* suggests yields are similar at nearly all maturities and, thus, there is more risk accepted for longer maturity but not additional yield. The flat yield curve is a situation to avoid. An *inverted yield curve*, where short rates are higher than long rates, suggests value in the short maturities.

Recent Trends Spotted

In 2008, the markets saw record levels of volatility in the bond markets, which generated a rush of interest to parts of the fixed-income market. Treasury yields were driven to historic lows by the demand, causing many to wonder if the market had entered a bubble. Few investors seemed to be considering whether it was worth it to hold a 30-year bond for a miniscule 3%–4% yield or T-bills that actually had negative yield! In the corporate markets, it was quite a different story as corporate bond yields soared. Some high quality corporate bonds showed yields in excess of 10% while some high yield corporates were as high as 20%. Corporate bond funds and ETFs will decline in value, but their yields will increase.

Here's a possible scenario: The markets regain stability, the rush to Treasuries ends, and prices fall (yields rise). This could be the beginning of a bubble bursting in that markets cause a downtrend in returns. In the corporate and municipal markets, the oversold conditions and high yield will attract investors, and prices and returns will rebound. Some of this was already seen in early 2009. Later, if inflation picks up due to the immense deficits the United States is facing, rates will most likely rise as well, again impacting returns.

If you believe that this could happen, then there are a few options available to you:

- Don't own individual bond issues unless you plan on holding them to maturity.
- Have a sell point for bond funds and ETFs—use the 200-day moving average.
- Identify in advance those ETFs that may be more sensitive to rising rates, such as long maturity funds.

Bonds might be a completely different animal than the rest of the market, but they aren't exempt from the trend lines.

Taxes and Municipal Bond Trends

Another trend under way is higher taxes. The economic recession put a heavy burden on both the federal and state governments. To help balance these budgets, taxes are trending higher, especially for higher tax bracket investors (see Figure 12.3). One way to take advantage of this trend is via the *tax-exempt bond market*. Since yields in this market are federally tax exempt; their value increases as taxes rise. For ·those bonds in your home state, you get exemption on the federal and state level.

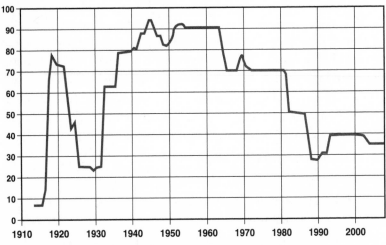

Figure 12.3 *Marginal tax rate in top bracket (percent), 1910–2000*

One of the growing segments of the ETF marketplace is *municipal bond funds*. As of early 2009, there were only a few. Although the returns they generate aren't as explosive, they can be appealing because their income is federally tax-free and, in some cases, federal and state if the bonds are from your home state. They tend to yield less than taxable bonds on an absolute yield basis, but when you calculate the taxable equivalent yield, you'll see they can be very attractive.

To evaluate and compare tax-exempt yield, the standard comparison is done by calculating a *taxable equivalent yield (TEY)*. The TEY simply describes what taxable return must be achieved to equate to a particular tax-exempt yield, taking into consideration the investor's tax bracket. The simplest TEY is calculated by dividing the tax-exempt yield by 1, minus the investor's federal tax bracket.

Here's an example of a 5%, longer maturity, municipal yield assuming a top current federal rate of 35%:

$$5.0\% / (1 - 0.35\%) = 7.69\% = TEY$$

On a federal income basis, this means an investor must receive 7.69% in a taxable investment to equal that of the 5% municipal investment. This does not take into consideration the possible upgrade in quality of using municipal bonds over a more volatile corporate bond.

As an investment vehicle, municipal ETFs have a lot going for them. Generally, fees are about half of a municipal bond fund—0.20% to 0.40%—compared to 0.50% to 0.80%. Even if it's just one-half percent you're saving, that's a lot of money. Unlike government bonds which are highly liquid, municipal bonds can have periods of illiquidity where prices become volatile. This was seen in several periods in 2007 and 2008. However, these "dislocations" provide opportunity for investors to capture high exempt yields if they have a longer time horizon.

If you can't decide whether to go tax-free or taxable when it comes to bonds, there are a number of calculators to help you decide what you need. A good one is located at www.investingbonds.com/calcs/taxcalculator/taxcalcform.aspx. You could also consult your accountant for more information.

High-Yield Opportunity

As mentioned earlier, the high yield bond market went through a burst bubble in the early 1990s that led to long-term gains. After getting hit hard in 2007 and 2008 as fears of rising default rates prevailed, yields soared to 20%, crushing the return and the prices. However, as the economy rebounds in the coming years, these more speculative companies should also stabilize. As this happens, their bond yields could become very attractive to investors willing to invest in this market. The result could be returns on par with the equity market. Again, ETFs provide a simple and liquid access point to this more volatile market sector.

Fixed-Income ETFs

Until 2007, the market for fixed-income ETFs was fairly limited. Investors had to content themselves with tracking brand-name indexes (S&P 500, NASDAQ, and the like) before tackling the new and innovative types of ETFs that track commodities, currency, and, eventually, bonds. And it's true that ETFs typically are used more heavily for stock investments.

iShares was the first provider on the scene that investors could turn to for access to the bond market via ETFs. The provider continued to expand the number of funds it offered, and the fixed-income ETF universe more than doubled in less than two years. Competitors have caught on, and other ETF providers are frequently adding new funds to the pipeline. Fixed-income ETFs are just another example of how ETF providers are actively seeking new ways to explore what ETFs are able to do.

What's true for ETFs in general also holds true for bond ETFs: They still have low trading costs and exchange traded prices, and they enable investors to continue to diversify their portfolios. One of the best selling points about bond funds, in particular, is how cost-effectively they manage to target what can be an expensive segment of the market.

You should consider three main points with indexed bond ETFs:

1. **Costs are generally low.** Expense ratios for bond ETFs are 0.15–0.20%, depending on a few factors such as credits and maturities in the bond index. But the more specialized a bond ETF becomes, the higher the expense ratio goes, simply because the fancier you get, the more upkeep is required. Additionally, many kinds of individual bonds can be bought only in $5,000 increments, so getting this kind of exposure to individual bonds easily and cheaply is a real challenge.

2. **Additional trading costs could be passed on to you.** As with mutual funds, the annual ETF expense ratio doesn't include trading costs the managers rack up. And they aren't doing it for free. Even though the transaction charges at your broker could be small, many trades do add up. However, if done correctly, these costs should be minimal.

3. **Distributions should be primarily interest income.** In looking at the distribution history of iShares' broad-based indexed bond ETF, iShares Aggregate Bond (AGG), no short- or long-term capital gains have been distributed; only interest has come back. But don't get excited: This doesn't mean that no capital gains will be distributed in the future. It will still hold true, however, that the meaningful distributions on indexed bond ETFs will be interest, not capital gains.

Who Wants Bonds?

Most bond investors are in it for the long haul. If you've got major life events coming up for which you'll need a lot of money (you *do* want to retire, don't you?), you might consider adding bond investments to your portfolio as well. They're considered a fairly safe and, if done well, low-cost way to invest in your own peace of mind. A typical formula is to subtract your age from 100 to get the percentage of your portfolio that should be allocated to stocks; the remainder would go to bonds. For example, a 30-year-old would have a 70% allocation to stocks, 30% to bonds.

Just as bonds come in an array of styles and risk levels, so do bond ETFs:

- **Broad exposure**—These generally track a benchmark for the broad U.S. investment-grade bond market. A good, cheap way to play this market is through the Vanguard Total Bond Market (BND). It tracks the Barclays Capital U.S. Aggregate Bond Index. (www.vanguard.com)

- **Short term**—These ETFs allow you to be cautious toward a potential increase in interest rates. A possible play here could be the iShares MBS Bond Fund (MBB). It tracks the Barclays Capital U.S. MBS Fixed-Rate Index. (www.ishares. com)

- **Municipal bond**—One play here could be the iShares S&P National Municipal Bond (MUB). It tracks the S&P National Municipal Bond Index.

- **Corporate bond**—The iShares iBoxx $ Investment Grade Corporate Bond (LQD) tracks the iBoxx $ Liquid Investment-Grade Index. It holds bonds rated investment grade.

- **High-yield bond**—These bonds can be found in ETFs such as the PowerShares High Yield Corporate Bond (PHB).

It tracks the Wachovia High-Yield Bond Index. Its holdings consist of high-yield bonds. (www.invescopowershares.com)

How to Choose Bond ETFs

Buying an ETF that tracks a bond index is a simple, low-cost way to invest in bonds just as you would buy a single stock—that is, in one simple transaction. As with other investment vehicles, you have a choice as to how broad or focused you want to be. You can choose one of the bond funds listed previously, or you can invest in one of the total bond market ETFs.

If you're thinking about getting into bond ETFs, they can be a secure investment tool, as long as you do your homework and are mindful of the risks previously listed. Bond ETFs offer some of the best diversification out there when it comes to investing in bonds. In addition, you get the combined diversification and liquidity because the ETF is traded on the public exchange instead of through an underwriter. These ETFs are a fantastic way to get wide exposure to a market with considerable risk, but also with potential reward if played well. Bond ETFs are the better choice if you're seeking flexible trading and more transparency—you can find out what your portfolio looks like at any hour of the day online. With an index bond mutual fund, that information is available only semiannually.

How do the bond ETFs address the issue of liquidity? They use what's called *representative sampling,* meaning that the fund tracks only a sufficient number of bonds to represent the entire index. The bonds in the sample are usually the largest and most liquid. As an example, the Lehman Aggregate Bond Index has more than 6,000 bonds, but the Barclays iShares Lehman Aggregate Bond Fund (AGG) has just a little more than 100 of those bonds.

chapter 13

Getting Leverage in the Markets

During the last several bear markets, you might have been well served by reducing your exposure to equities. A number of investors—perhaps even you—decided to "short" the market instead of exiting entirely. But why go short?

Short selling, as it pertains to stocks, is the selling of a security you do not own.

It works like this: Say you believe that Company A is about to take a big hit and its shares are going to lose value. You call your broker and tell him that you want to sell 100 shares of Company A (which you do not own) at $50 per share. The broker will borrow those shares from another client's account and effectively lend you the shares to sell short, and your account will be credited with the sales price of 100 shares, minus commission. In a best-case scenario, those shares lose value. You then purchase 100 shares at the lower price, say $20, to make the transaction whole, gaining $30 per share, less any fees that apply.

Why would you want to short stocks, or anything else? The theory is that by shorting stocks, investors can potentially make money when the stock loses value. This contrasts with "going long," which is simply when you take a position with the expectation that the price will rise.

Short selling can help you accomplish a few goals:

• To hedge long positions during challenging market conditions or during a market correction if, for whatever reason, you don't want to sell your current position. For example, if you're long on oil but it's correcting, you could hold your long position and hedge it by buying a short oil fund as a temporary measure. What are some scenarios in which you would not want to sell? Sometimes selling might trigger a tax event, or you only want to capitalize on a temporary market move, but not one so great that you feel it's necessary to sell your position.

- To make specific bets on the market. For example, if you believe that financials have been in a bubble and might see some declines soon, you might take a short position and attempt to profit from the downturn.

The Long and Short of ETFs

Long and short ETFs have been around since 2006, but 2008 was their coming-out party. That year was the worst for the stock market since 1931, and the worst year ever in the 15-year history of ETFs.

Many investors, not content to cash out their positions and wait out the downturn on the sidelines, sent leveraged and inverse ETFs soaring in assets as they sought to make money even through a downturn. This wound up making these funds 19 of the top-performing 20 ETFs for that year.

Funds are now available for investors who want more octane in their portfolios. Leveraged ETFs allow investors to go two times and three times long or short on the markets, meaning that instead of simply moving in the opposite direction of the index they track, they move either 200% or 300% the opposite.

Although the trend following strategy works best with traditional ETFs, that doesn't mean it can't be used when it comes to funds that double or triple the movements of the market. The key, however, is to watch these funds daily, because these funds are high-octane.

Short (or inverse) ETFs use derivatives to profit from a decline in value of their underlying benchmarks. Investing in them is similar to holding short positions, but there is one big advantage to holding them over individual stocks: ease. Anyone can use short ETFs, if they choose to do so, by simply purchasing the fund. No complicated borrowing is involved; no margin accounts are needed.

Leveraged and short ETFs instead achieve their exposure this way: A long fund, such as the ProShares Ultra Financials (UYG), seeks to double the returns of the Dow Jones U.S. Financials Index. That means when the index goes up, your returns should double that.

If a fund looking to double that index has $100, then ProShares would want to have baskets of stocks, futures contracts, and swaps in the fund that give it roughly $200 exposure to that same index. The baskets of stocks give dollar-for-dollar exposure; futures contracts and swaps are inherently leveraged, therefore it isn't necessary to put down $1 to get $1 worth of exposure.

A short, double-short, or triple short fund seeks to provide the opposite of the index, twice the opposite, or three times the opposite. Examples of these are the UltraShort MSCI EAFE ProShares (EFU) and the Direxion Daily Small Cap Bear 3x (TZA). Shorts work in a similar way to funds that take double-long positions, with one key difference: They don't buy long positions because they are short funds.

Naturally, going short and leveraged comes with certain risks investors should be mindful of:

- **These funds can be hypervolatile**—Any fund that doubles or triples market movements in either direction can see big swings, even in one day. Not only do these funds frequently go back and forth above their 200-day moving averages, but it's not unusual to see swings of 20% or more in a single day.
- **These are not buy-and-hold tools**—Short and leveraged funds are meant as short-term positions, nothing more. Over

time, they tend to stray from their benchmarks. On a daily basis, these funds track according to their stated objectives. But over time, because they reset daily, their performance won't be exactly the opposite of the indexes they're shorting.

Because of the volatility in these funds, it's important to mind the 200-day moving average. It's also important to understand that you'll be buying and selling them fairly quickly as a matter of course. Not only do they frequently go back and forth above their 200-day moving averages, it's not unusual to see swings of 20% or more in a single day.

ETFs AND Options

ETFs have helped simplify many things about the market, and options are no exception. Whereas managing stock options can be a juggling act, using options on ETFs helps cut down on the paperwork, expense, and time-consuming tracking.

Options are the right to buy (known as a **call**) or the right to sell (known as a **put**) a security at a certain price before a certain date. There is no obligation to buy or sell, though.

While the ETFs themselves have value, these rights also have value and are bought and sold on exchanges. Their prices shift just as the fortunes of the underlying stocks or ETFs do, as well as in accordance with the time that's left on the contract.

Calls tend to be speculative, because the options can expire worthless. They can also rocket up dramatically, however, and leave a buyer vulnerable to big losses.

If you want protection on the losses you sustain, purchasing puts for an ETF gives you the opportunity to sell it if the price drops below the strike price in the specified period of time. If you buy it alone, it could expire worthless. If you sell it alone, it exposes you to bigger losses because the underlying holdings could fall sharply in value.

Options activity on ETFs isn't frequently discussed as a strategy when it comes to ETF discussions, probably because many think of options as complicated. It isn't the simplest thing, but it shouldn't be intimidating.

Many ETFs have options available on them. You can find a complete list at the Chicago Board Options Exchange (CBOE). As you begin to feel more comfortable with ETFs, you might find yourself looking to venture out and try more sophisticated strategies. What ETFs offer (transparency, low-cost, and so on) is really only the tip of the iceberg.

Options on ETFs can help generate additional income or protect portfolios from further losses. It's just a matter of knowing how to use them. The types of ETF options available span the range from the most widely traded ETFs based on major benchmarks, such as the SPDRS (SPY) and the Diamonds (DIA), as well as major sector and single-country ETFs. If you want to incorporate options into your strategy though, be sure that the options you're using are liquid and have tight spreads, because not all ETFs have liquid options available.

One factor to consider with options is the cost/benefit ratio. There are fees associated with buying and selling ETFs, and adding options into the mix adds another layer of fees, known as **premiums**. If you're paying too much to use options, it may not be worth it. Think about the transaction fees you're incurring—they can be justified if you're faced with selling out an entire position, which would generate its own fees. Consider the taxes as well. Is it more beneficial to hold on to your position when selling means that you'd incur capital gains? Or is it more beneficial to pick up an option, knowing that income from them doesn't have low, long-term tax gain treatment?

Pumping Up Returns

In 2006, ProShares was first to market with a new line of not only ETFs that allowed investors to get ETFs doing the opposite of whatever the market did, but also some leveraged ETFs that did *twice* the opposite of whatever the market did. For example, if you had an inverse ETF for the S&P 500, if the S&P went up 1%, your ETF would go down 1%, and vice versa. With a double short, if the S&P went up 1%, your ETF would go down 2%, and, again, vice versa. Double leverage simply does whatever the market does, times two. If the S&P goes up 2%, the double leverage ETF goes up 4%. Call it the stock market's version of "double down." In late 2008, Direxion grabbed the attention of the market by launching a line of *triple* leveraged ETFs. Given the volatility, they were an overnight hit with investors.

As of early 2009, dozens of short and leveraged ETFs gave investors the chance to make plays on major indexes, sectors, and even commodities and currencies. Here I've listed some of the funds available, along with what they seek to correspond to:

- **ProShares UltraShort S&P 500 (SDS)**—Twice the inverse of the daily performance of the S&P 500 Index (www.proshares.com)

- **ProShares Ultra Consumer Services (UCC)**—Twice the daily performance of the Dow Jones U.S. Consumer Services Index

- **Rydex 2x S&P Select Sector Technology (RTG)**—Twice the daily performance of the Technology Select Sector Index (www.rydexfunds.com)

- **Rydex Inverse 2x S&P MidCap 400 (RMS)**—Twice the inverse of the daily performance of the Mid Cap 400 Index

- **Direxion Technology Bear 3x Shares (TYP)**—Three times the inverse of the daily performance of the Russell 1000 Technology Index (www.direxionshares.com)

- **Direxion Developed Markets Bull 3x Shares (DZK)—**
  Three times the daily performance of the MSCI EAFE Index

WHAT'S THE BEEF WITH SHORT AND LEVERAGED ETFs?

With popularity tends to come a lot of criticism and nit-picking. Leveraged ETFs are no exception. Some pundits believe these specialized ETFs have increased market volatility in the last hour of trading. But many investors and people in the media are having trouble getting their arms around the truth. The SEC has been looking closely at these funds and have had dialogue and visits with ETF providers who are offering them. Here are the facts:

Myth: Leveraged ETFs are too readily available, and average investors will hurt themselves.

Fact: What's wrong with choices? We're all adults here. Investors deserve to have options—and the more, the better. Give investors some credit. I know our readers on ETF Trends, and they're a smart, educated, affluent bunch. It's up to you and me to get the necessary education so we don't shoot ourselves in the foot.

Furthermore, the fund companies that issue leveraged ETFs readily admit that their funds aren't for everyone. They're very open about the risks. As much as the fund companies want to make money, they also want their investors to be successful. It behooves them to help investors do that. As Jason Zweig of *The Wall Street Journal* noted in his weekly column, it's all about understanding risk and knowing what you're getting into with these funds.

Another point to consider is that it's hard to know exactly who's buying these funds, but based on the volume being traded, it's largely institutional. True, anyone can buy them, but the big players are likely the ones buying them at this point, so their accessibility is probably moot for now.

Myth: They exist so investors can sidestep margins rules.

Fact: It's really not that sinister. Before leveraged ETFs, investors had to borrow from a broker to short with credit, then have a required amount of reserve capital before doing so. These limitations don't exist with leveraged ETFs, but I doubt that most investors are arching their eyebrows and laughing wickedly at the thought of sidestepping margins rules.

The less exciting truth is that these funds have simply made it easier for average investors to employ a strategy they might not have had access to before. Additionally, margin rules were set up to protect banks, not investors, so this argument doesn't hold much water. Investors can lose only what they put into these funds.

Myth: Leveraged funds brought the market down.

Fact: A lot of things make it difficult for the government to save financials, and it isn't right or fair to put the blame on the shoulders of leveraged ETFs. Trading and interest in them have undoubtedly increased, but billions of shares trade hands each day in funds of all types.

A small fraction of that is leveraged ETFs, yet they seem to be getting a far greater percentage of the blame. One industry expert points out that if you look at the net assets in both the long and short funds, the levels are net long in most of the fund pairings most of the time. If anything, leveraged ETFs are having a positive effect on the market.

Myth: They're not buy-and-hold investments.

Fact: Well, that's true. But this isn't exactly news—many leveraged ETF investors have been able to successfully hedge their portfolios for short-term periods. The ETF providers readily acknowledge that these types of funds are meant to hedge risk; they're not funds around which investors should plan their retirement.

Myth: Leveraged ETFs just don't work.

Fact: Leveraged ETFs operate exactly as they should: They reset daily. Over a period of time, you'll see internal compounding affect the returns. This isn't a flaw in the funds—this is a mathematical fact that is impossible to avoid. If you invested in a leveraged ETF over a period of months and the market went down 20%, a 2x short leveraged ETF wouldn't go up exactly 40%.

The SEC ultimately will find that there's nothing illegal or underhanded about these products. They're doing what they're supposed to do, they've proven immensely popular, and the SEC cannot impose limits or consider doing away with such innovative products.

chapter 14

Conclusion: Let's Get to Work

At last, here we are. If you've made it this far, it tells me that you're motivated and ready to put this strategy to work. You're ready to stop losing money to emotional decisions and hunches, and you're ready to start letting the market's activity dictate what you buy, when you buy it, and when you sell it.

I want you to walk away from reading this book feeling like you're a much more knowledgeable and more confident investor. I hope you now realize how crucial it is to use a no-nonsense, unemotional strategy that requires a good amount of discipline on both the buy and sell sides of the investment equation. I'm rooting for you, because you can do this. Thousands of investors have done it, and I know you can, too.

But you still have some questions to ask yourself, because a strategy like this requires a strict discipline to work most effectively. Just as watching what you eat only 50% of the time will not lead to weight loss, neither will following an investment discipline 50% of the time lead to profits or success. You've got to be all in, 100% committed, and it can be done. It's what I do for my own money management clients, and I do it with ETFs.

Are you comfortable enough to manage your own assets by monitoring and following the trends with the 200-day moving average? If so, you might want to start slowly with a portion of your portfolio and add to your positions as your confidence strengthens. Or you could always "practice" this strategy with any of the web sites that provide tracking capability and portfolio construction, see how it works with your own eyes, and determine from your success where to go from there.

Not every trade is a winning trade. In fact, during some market conditions, every other trade can end up being a losing trade. But even during difficult times, if the losing trades are small (due to a stop-loss strategy), those winning trades can be much more substantial.

Make no mistake: You can do this yourself. But it also requires a firm and unbending discipline. Sometimes you're going to have to do something you find difficult, such as buying when you don't feel emotionally ready to do so, or selling when you aren't prepared to let go. If you stick to following the trends, there are many tools available today to help you implement this strategy, such as the following.

- **Online brokerage firms**—Because trend following is becoming a more acceptable mainstream strategy, brokerages such as TD Ameritrade, E-Trade, Scottrade, Fidelity, and Schwab enable you to set individual stop-losses on your positions and receive alerts when a certain price is hit. You can also use the tools I outlined in Chapter 6, "Tools You Can Use," to assist you while your account is with an online broker.

- **Financial advisors**—If becoming a self-directed investor doesn't sound appealing to you, you can always defer to a financial advisor. The downside to this approach, though, is that most advisors and brokerages will advise you to use an asset-allocation model following a buy-and-hold strategy. It's too much work for them to follow trends and take the time to monitor ETFs regularly. Doing this might take you several hours a week, but with so many clients, advisors simply can't devote that much time to individuals.

Chances are, you are reading this book because you had a bad money-losing experience with an advisor, or you have made mistakes yourself that wound up being very costly to you. In either case, you have to be your own best advocate.

This is the best time ever to be an investor. You have access to more information, more tools, and you have more choices than any other generation before you has had.

Switching from Mutual Funds to ETFs

Whether you're an individual investor or an advisor, you too can make the switch to ETFs. It's simply a matter of education, and once you see the advantages of making this change, you'll find that the transition is a smooth one. I speak from personal experience.

I use ETFs in my own advisory firm because of their great advantages: transparency (and the ease of accessing this information), low cost, capability to provide instant diversification, and the number of options I have when using them.

When I started my firm in 1996, ETFs were just getting off the ground and there were relatively few available. Mutual funds were firmly entrenched as portfolio staples for most advisory firms. During the '90s, I looked for markets and managers who outperformed the conventional markets like small-cap and international funds. But in the late '90s, I often ran into issues with the best managers as they closed their funds to new money or imposed heavy redemption fees on shareholders who sold their funds.

Because of my tactical investing discipline, mutual funds weren't working with my overall plan. I needed more liquidity; but in the late '90s, there were times when I had to use lesser-performing funds in order to avoid the prospect of potentially paying higher early redemption fees.

In the early 2000s, I looked closely at ETFs, because they made perfect sense for my investment style. The advantages were obvious:

There were many asset class choices; they cost less than mutual funds; they were liquid; I knew exactly what the underlying holders were; and they were tax-efficient.

One of the biggest hurdles I faced was educating clients about the advantages of ETFs. Today, investors are more familiar with the concept of ETFs, but if they haven't owned them before, there is an education process. Clients who have been accustomed to owning only mutual funds have to be educated on the fact that they'll pay transaction fees at the brokerage level but the underlying expenses are much less.

When I made the transition to ETF, there were barely 100 ETFs; today, there are more than 700 available. Making the transition was simple and beneficial to my clients and my practice.

Working with Your Advisor

Having a financial advisor is just like any other relationship. It has to work for you: You have to feel comfortable, and it has to be beneficial and rewarding.

If your money is being professionally managed, you can at least question your current advisor and "make suggestions" on your behalf, as a friend of mine did. This friend is pretty diligent in checking his statements and did so during 2008 as he slowly watched his balance decline. He went back and read Chapter 12 of my first book, *iMoney: Profitable ETF Strategies for Every Investor* (Lydon and Wasik, 2008, FT Press). This chapter included information on the rules everyone should follow, the 200-day moving average, and trend following. Afterward, he called his advisor and asked him bluntly, "Why didn't you take some money off the table?" Then he told him to read Chapter 12 of my first book.

Remember, though, that your advisor is not always going to listen or be open to a shift in strategy, and you have to be prepared to make a switch to one who has a philosophy similar to your own. Many advisors have their own strategies that they have been using for years, and they can't custom-make them for each client. Choosing an advisor is much like choosing a therapist: You've got to find one with whom you work well.

There are many things to consider when you're choosing the person who's going to manage your money and lead you into your "golden years." Here are my top five:

1. Does your advisor stay in touch to your satisfaction? Some clients are content with quarterly letters; others like a personal phone call or office meeting. Some clients want hand-holding and reassurance during tough periods. Whatever your communication needs happen to be, does your advisor meet them?

2. Do you understand the quarterly statements you receive? Are the fonts, language, and charts clear and easy to read? Does what they're saying make sense to you?

3. If you're really concerned about something, does your advisor listen to you and work to address your concerns? While advisors won't shift their entire investing philosophy to accommodate one client, smart ones know when to make certain concessions to clients whose assets are at stake.

4. Does your advisor do what's best for you and your portfolio instead of focusing on brand names and pushing particular products? Advisors should be investing money on what's right in accordance with his or her philosophy and acting in the client's best interest.

5. What are the fees like? Calculate them over time to see what you're spending. If you think the fees are too high,

speak up. Fee-based advisors might be better, since you pay a specified rate and always know what you're getting.

Wrap-Up

My firm's web site, ETF Trends (www.etftrends.com), can be viewed as an extension of this book. I have charting, news, forums, and educational resources you can use to further your education on ETFs and the trend following discipline. Feel free to stop by anytime to share your experiences or ask questions.

The key to success with this plan is making a commitment for a reasonable period of time. Since trends don't appear overnight, the success you'll attain won't happen overnight. But if you stick to your newfound discipline over time, you'll be rewarded.

I hope that I've given you the information, tools, and support you need to go forward and become a successful and profitable investor. I'm on your side.

Good luck!

Glossary

alpha

A measure of performance on a risk-adjusted basis. Alpha takes the volatility (price risk) of a mutual fund and compares its risk-adjusted performance to a benchmark index. The excess return of the fund relative to the return of the benchmark index is a fund's alpha.

bear market

A market in which the prices of securities are falling. A downturn of at least 15–20% in more than one index is considered to be the start of a bear market.

beta

A measure of the volatility, or systematic risk, of a security or a portfolio in comparison to the market as a whole.

blend

Also known as a hybrid fund. A category of equity mutual funds with portfolios made up of both value and growth stocks.

bond

A debt security in which the issuer owes the holder debt. Depending on the bond's terms, the issuer is obligated to pay the holder the debt, plus interest, on a specified date (known as maturity).

bubble

A cycle characterized by rapid expansion followed by a contraction.

bull market

A market in which securities are rising.

buy and hold

An investment strategy in which stocks are bought and then held for a long period, regardless of the market's fluctuations.

call

Buyers of call options bet that a stock will be worth more than the price set by the option (the strike price), plus the price they pay for the option itself.

capital gain

Profit taxed at rates that could be lower than rates on ordinary income; the result of the sale of a capital asset.

closing price

Price of the last transaction of a particular stock completed during a day's trading session on an exchange.

commodity

A product used in commerce and traded on a commodity exchange.

Consumer Price Index (CPI)

A measure that examines the weighted average of prices of a basket of consumer goods and services, such as transportation, food, and medical care. The CPI is calculated by averaging price changes for each item in the predetermined basket of goods; the goods are weighted according to their importance. Changes in CPI are used to assess price changes associated with the cost of living.

corporate bond

Debt obligation issued by corporations.

correction

A drop of at least 10% in an index or market, often seen as a sign of a healthy market when part of a larger trend.

credit quality

One of the principal criteria for judging the investment quality of a bond or bond mutual fund. As the term implies, credit quality informs investors of a bond or bond portfolio's creditworthiness, or risk of default.

cyclical stock
The evolution of a stock's price, from an early uptrend to a price high and eventually to a downtrend. The stock cycle is a buy-and-sell cycle that occurs over several years and has four stages: accumulation, markup, distribution, and markdown.

day trading
Establishing and liquidating the same position or positions within one day's trading.

debenture
A type of debt instrument that is not secured by physical asset or collateral. Debentures are backed only by the general creditworthiness and reputation of the issuer. Both corporations and governments frequently issue this type of bond to secure capital. Similar to other types of bonds, debentures are documented in an indenture.

diversification
A risk-management technique that mixes a wide variety of investments within a portfolio.

dotcom
A company that embraces the Internet as the key component in its business.

Dow Jones Industrial Average (DJIA)
A price-weighted average of 30 significant stocks traded on the New York Stock Exchange and the NASDAQ. Charles Dow invented the DJIA in 1896.

downtrend

Describes the price movement of a financial asset when the overall direction is downward. A formal downtrend occurs when each successive peak and trough is lower than the ones earlier in the trend.

earnings per share (EPS)

A company's profit divided by the number of shares of outstanding common stock.

exchange-traded fund (ETF)

A basket of stocks tracking an underlying index, commodity, or currency. ETFs are traded like stocks daily and on an exchange.

exchange-traded note (ETN)

A type of unsecured, unsubordinated debt security that was first issued by Barclays Bank PLC. This type of debt security differs from other types of bonds and notes in three ways: ETN returns are based on the performance of a market index minus applicable fees, no period coupon payments are distributed, and no principal protections exist.

expense ratio

A measure of what it costs an investment company to operate a mutual fund. An expense ratio is determined through an annual calculation, in which a fund's operating expenses are divided by the average dollar value of its assets under management. Operating expenses are taken out of a fund's assets and lower the return to a fund's investors.

forex

The market in which participants buy, sell, exchange, and speculate on currencies. The forex market is made up of banks, commercial companies, central banks, investment management firms, hedge funds, and retail forex brokers and investors. The currency market is considered to be the largest financial market in the world, processing trillions of dollars' worth of transactions each day.

fund

A pool of money normally set apart for a purpose—for example, a pension fund to provide pensions.

future

A financial contract obligating the buyer to purchase an asset (or the seller to sell an asset), such as a physical commodity or a financial instrument, at a predetermined future date and price.

growth investing

Emphasis on stocks on the way up, with potential for greater-than-average returns.

hedging

Making an investment to reduce the risk of adverse price movements in an asset. Normally, a hedge consists of taking an offsetting position in a related security, such as a futures contract.

index

A group of securities representing a specific market or portion of a market. Among the best-known indexes are the Standard & Poor's 500 and the Dow Jones Industrial Average.

index fund

A mutual fund that tracks an index. ETFs are one example of an index fund.

initial margin

The percentage of the purchase price of securities (that can be purchased on margin) that the investor must pay for with his own cash or marginable securities.

initial public offering (IPO)

The first sale of stock by a private company to the public. IPOs are often issued by smaller, younger companies seeking the capital to expand, but they can also be issued by large, privately owned companies looking to become publicly traded.

interest rate risk

A type of risk that asserts that the characteristics of interest rate fluctuation are variable (instead of constant) over a period of time. Although interest rates are expected to fluctuate over the period of an investment, the probability of an interest rate change is not always constant, nor is the magnitude of the volatility of interest rate changes.

inverse ETF

An exchange-traded fund (ETF) that is constructed by using various derivatives for the purpose of profiting from a decline in the value of an underlying benchmark. Investing in these ETFs is similar to holding various short positions, or using a combination of advanced investment strategies to profit from falling prices.

junk bond

A bond rated BB or lower because of its high default risk. Also known as a "high-yield bond" or "speculative bond."

large-cap

Companies with a market capitalization of $10 billion or more.

leveraging

Using various financial instruments or borrowed capital, such as margin, to increase the potential return of an investment.

limit-buy

An order placed with a brokerage to buy a set number of shares at a specified price or better. Limit orders also allow an investor to limit the length of time an order can be outstanding before it is canceled.

liquidity
The capability to buy or sell securities in the market without the asset's price being affected or an asset's quick conversion to cash.

maintenance margin
The minimum amount of equity that must be maintained in a margin account.

margin call
A broker's demand on an investor using margin to deposit additional money or securities so that the margin account is brought up to the minimum maintenance margin.

market timing
A strategy in which a trader takes advantage of the different closing times of markets around the world.

marketable security
Very liquid securities that can be converted into cash quickly at a reasonable price, because they tend to have maturities of less than one year. Furthermore, the rate at which these securities can be bought or sold has little effect on their prices.

micro-cap
Companies with a market capitalization of $250 million or lower.

mid-cap
Companies with a market capitalization of between $1 billion and $8 billion.

minimum margin
The initial amount required to be deposited in a margin account before trading on margin or selling short.

money market

The global financial market for short-term borrowing and lending money, typically for three years or less. The securities in a money market can be U.S. government bonds, Treasury bills, and commercial paper from banks and companies.

moving average (MA)

An indicator frequently used in technical analysis, showing the average value of a security's price over a set period. Moving averages generally measure momentum and define areas of possible support and resistance.

municipal bond

A debt security issued by a state, municipality, or county to finance its capital expenditures. Municipal bonds are exempt from federal taxes and from most state and local taxes, especially if you live in the state where the bond is issued.

mutual fund

Pool of money that is managed by an investment company. Mutual funds come in two types: no-load funds and open-end funds.

NASDAQ Composite Index

Measures all NASDAQ domestic- and international-based common type stocks listed on the NASDAQ Stock Market. Because it is so broad-based, with approximately 3,000 companies, the NASDAQ Composite Index is one of the most widely quoted major market indexes.

NASDAQ Stock Market

Recognized around the globe as the largest U.S. stock exchange—listing more companies, trading more volume, and handling more IPOs than any other U.S. exchange.

NASDAQ-100 Index

One of the most widely followed benchmarks in the world, it is comprised of 100 of the largest domestic and international nonfinancial securities listed on the NASDAQ Stock Market. The NASDAQ-100 Index is only the second index to have crossed the 5/25 milestone; 600 million contracts traded/$25 trillion in notional value.

net asset value (NAV)
Calculated daily, the total value of the portfolio of a fund minus its liabilities.

no-load mutual fund
A type of mutual fund in which shares are sold without a commission or sales charge.

nonmarketable security
Any type of security that is difficult to buy or sell because it does not trade on a normal market or exchange. These types of securities trade over-the-counter (OTC) or in a private transaction. Finding a party with which to transact business is often difficult; in some cases, these securities can't be resold due to regulations surrounding the security.

NYSE
A stock exchange based in New York City, which is considered the largest equities-based exchange in the world based on total market capitalization of its listed securities.

Nikkei 225
The leading and most-respected index of Japanese stocks. It is a price-weighted index comprised of Japan's top 225 blue-chip companies on the Tokyo Stock Exchange. The Nikkei is equivalent to the Dow Jones Industrial Average Index in the United States. It was called the Nikkei Dow Jones Stock Average from 1975 to 1985.

open-end mutual fund
A type of mutual fund that does not have restrictions on the amount of shares the fund will issue. If demand is high enough, the fund will

continue to issue shares no matter how many investors there are. Open-end funds also buy back shares when investors want to sell.

option
Part of a class of securities called derivatives, which means these securities derive their value from the worth of an underlying investment. An option gives the buyer the right, but not the obligation, to buy (call) or sell an asset (put) at a set price on or before a given date. Investors, not companies, issue options.

over-the-counter (OTC)
Any security traded somewhere other than on a formal exchange.

pink sheets
A daily publication assembled by the National Quotation Bureau to provide bid and ask prices of OTC securities.

price-to-book ratio (P/B)
A ratio comparing a stock's market value to its book value, calculated by dividing the closing price of the stock by the latest quarter's book value per share.

price-to-earnings ratio (P/E)
The valuation ratio of a company's current share price compared to its per-share earnings.

put
Buyers of put options bet that the stock's price will drop below the price set by the option.

quant investing
A fund that selects securities based on quantitative analysis. Managers build computer models to select investments.

risk-adjusted return
A concept that refines an investment's return by measuring how much risk is involved in producing that return, which is generally expressed as a number or rating.

Roth 401(k)
An employer-sponsored investment savings account that is funded with after-tax money. After the investor reaches age 59.5, withdrawals of any money from the account (including investment gains) are tax-free. Unlike the Roth IRA, the Roth 401(k) has no income limitations for investors who want to participate—anyone, regardless of income, is allowed to invest up to the contribution limit into the plan.

Roth IRA
An individual retirement plan that bears many similarities to the traditional IRA, but contributions are not tax-deductible and qualified distributions are tax-free. Similar to other retirement plan accounts, nonqualified distributions from a Roth IRA could be subject to a penalty upon withdrawal.

R-squared
A statistical measure that represents the percentage of a fund or security's movements that can be explained by movements in a benchmark index. For fixed-income securities, the benchmark is the T-bill. For equities, the benchmark is the S&P 500.

Russell 2000
An index measuring the performance of the 2,000 smallest companies in the Russell 3000 Index, which is made up of 3,000 of the biggest U.S. stocks. The Russell 2000 serves as a benchmark for small-cap stocks in the United States.

savings bond

A U.S. government savings bond that offers a fixed rate of interest over a fixed period of time. Many people find these bonds attractive because they are not subject to state or local income taxes. These bonds cannot be easily transferred and are non-negotiable.

Securities and Exchange Commission (SEC)

A government agency created under the Securities and Exchange Act of 1934, providing regulation in the securities markets.

security

Paper certificate (definitive security) or electronic record (book-entry security) evidencing ownership of equity (stocks) or debt obligations (bonds). Securities can be marketable or nonmarketable.

Sharpe ratio

A ratio developed by Nobel Laureate William F. Sharpe to measure risk-adjusted performance. The Sharpe ratio is calculated by subtracting the risk-free rate—such as that of the ten-year U.S. Treasury bond—from the rate of return for a portfolio and dividing the result by the standard deviation of the portfolio returns.

Short Sale Rule

A Securities and Exchange Commission (SEC) trading regulation that restricted short sales of stock from being placed on a downtick in the market price of the shares. The regulation was passed in 1938 to prevent selling shares short into a declining market; at the time, market mechanisms and liquidity couldn't be guaranteed to prevent panic-related share declines or outright manipulation.

short sell

Borrowing and then selling shares as an initial step, done on the assumption that the stock can be bought at a lower amount than the price at which the investor sold it. The sequence in a short position is sell, hold, buy, compared to that of a long position: buy, hold, sell.

sideways trend
Describes the horizontal price movement that occurs when the forces of supply and demand are nearly equal. A sideways trend is often regarded as a period of consolidation before the price continues in the direction of the previous move. A sideways price trend is also commonly known as a horizontal trend.

small-cap
Companies with a market capitalization of between $250 million and $2 billion.

spot price
The current price at which a particular commodity can be bought or sold at a specified time and place.

Standard & Poor's 500 (S&P 500)
An index of 500 stocks chosen for market size, liquidity, and industry grouping, among other factors. The S&P 500 is designed to be a leading indicator of U.S. equities and is meant to reflect the risk/return characteristics of the large-cap universe.

stock
A type of security that signifies ownership in a corporation and represents a claim on part of the corporation's assets and earnings.

stop-loss
An order placed with a broker to sell a security when it reaches a certain price. It is designed to limit an investor's loss on a security position. Also known as a stop order or stop-market order.

subprime
A type of loan that is offered at a rate above prime to individuals who do not qualify for prime-rate loans. Quite often, subprime borrowers are turned away from traditional lenders because of their low credit ratings or other factors that suggest they have a reasonable chance of defaulting on the debt repayment.

tracking error
A divergence between the price behavior of a position or a portfolio and the price behavior of a benchmark. This is often in the context of a hedge fund or mutual fund that did not work as effectively as intended, creating an unexpected profit or loss.

Treasury bond
A marketable, fixed-interest U.S. government debt security with a maturity of more than ten years. Treasury bonds make interest payments semiannually, and the income holders receive is taxed at only the federal level.

Treasury inflation-protected security (TIPS)
A U.S. Treasury note or bond pegged to the CPI, thus offering protection against inflation.

turnover rate
A measurement of how often the assets in a fund are bought and sold by its managers. It is calculated by dividing the total amount of new securities bought or sold (whichever is less) by the net asset value (NAV) of the fund.

trend
The general direction of a market or of the price of an asset. Trends can vary in length from short term, to intermediate, to long term.

Tokyo Securities & Stock Exchange (TSE)
Stock Exchange headquartered in Tokyo that was established on May 15, 1878, and began trading June 1, 1878.

ultra ETF
A class of exchange-traded funds (ETF) that uses leverage in an effort to achieve double the return of a set benchmark.

uptick
A transaction occurring at a price above the previous transaction. For an uptick to occur, a transaction price must be followed by an increased transaction price.

uptrend
Describes the price movement of a financial asset when the overall direction is upward. A formal uptrend occurs when each successive peak and trough is higher than the ones found earlier in the trend.

value investing
Focusing on stocks perceived to be available at bargain prices but exceptionally well managed.

volatility
A statistical measure of the dispersion of returns for a given security or market index. Volatility can be measured by using either the standard deviation or variance between returns from that same security or market index. Commonly, the higher the volatility, the riskier the security.

whipsaw
A condition in which a security's price heads in one direction but then is followed quickly by a movement in the opposite direction. The origin of the term comes from the push-and-pull action used by lumberjacks to cut wood with a type of saw of the same name.

yield

The income return on an investment. This refers to the interest or dividends received from a security. Yield is usually expressed annually as a percentage based on the investment's cost, its current market value, or its face value.

References and Resources

References

ABC News. "CEO Profiles—Madoff: One of Many Scammers? As the Economy Tanks, More and More Ponzi Schemes Come to Light." http://abcnews.go.com/Business/CEOProfiles/story?id=6701991&page=1

Abnormal Returns. "Cramer on ETF Proliferation." www.abnormalreturns. com/2006/07/12/cramer-on-etf-proliferation/

All Financial Matters. "What Is Fundamental Indexing?" http://allfinancialmatters.com/2006/11/14/what-is-fundamental-indexing/

American Stock Exchange. FAQ. www.amex.com/?href=/etf/FAQ/ et_etffaq.htm

Appleby, Denise. "ETFs for Your 401(k)." Investopedia. www.forbes.com/ personalfinance/retirementcollege/2007/07/25/etfs-401k-iras-pf-education-in_da_0725investopedia_inl.html

Arnott, Rob. "Rob Arnott Discusses the Fundamental Approach to Stock Market Indexing: Pimco Bonds." www.pimco.com/leftnav/product+focus/ 2005/arnott+fundamental+indexing+interview.htm

Associated Content. "Stock Market Trends." www.associatedcontent.com/ article/894951/stock_market_trends.html?page=4&cat=3

AXA Financial Protection. "Growth vs. Value: Two Approaches to Stock Selection." www.axaonline.com/rs/3p/sp/5040.html

Bailyn, Russell. "Indexes: What You Should Know." Russell Bailyn's Financial Planning Blog. www.russellbailyn.com/weblog/2007/04/ indexes_what_you_should_know.html

Barker, Bill. "70 Times Better Than the Next Microsoft." The Motley Fool. www.fool.com/investing/small-cap/2006/01/12/70-times-better-than-the-next-microsoft.aspx

Befumo, Randy. "A Lesson in Tax Efficiency." The Motley Fool. www.fool.com/school/mutualfunds/costs/efficiency.htm

Befumo, Randy, and Alex Schay. "History of the Dow." The Motley Fool. www.fool.com/ddow/historyofthedow5.htm

Bell, Heather. "XShares Launches First Lifecycle ETFs." IndexUniverse. www.indexuniverse.com/index.php?option=com_content&view=article&id=3172&Itemid=29

The Big Picture. "Buy and Hope Investing." www.ritholtz.com/blog/2009/02/buy-and-hope-investing/

Bloomberg.com. "Japan Returns to Pre-Thriller Era as Nikkei Slumps to '82 Level." www.bloomberg.com/apps/news?pid=20601101&refer=japan&sid=a_SuvQrkxAmU

Braun, Martin Z. "Barclay's Debuts State-Specific Exchange Traded Funds." Bloomberg Press. www.bloomberg.com/apps/news?pid=20601015&sid=a84uqZiGB2Oc&refer=munibonds

Burton, Jonathan. "Using ETFs for Bond Bets." *The Wall Street Journal* http://online.wsj.com/article/SB123308929930921057.html

BusinessWeek. "Emerging Markets, Beyond the Big Four." www.businessweek.com/magazine/content/05_52/b3965450.htm

BusinessWeek. "Smarter Ways to Make Currency Plays." www.businessweek.com/investor/content/feb2008/pi2008029_018751.htm?chan=top+news_top+news+index_businessweek+exclusives

Business Wire. "ProShares ETFs Pass $7 Billion in Assets." www.businesswire.com/portal/site/google/index.jsp?ndmViewId=news_view&newsId=20070809005029&newsLang=en

Buy and Hold, A Division of Freedom Communications. "Dissolving the Moving Averages Mystery." www.buyandhold.com/bh/en/education/mom/linda/2007/mom302.html

Caplinger, Dan. "The Long and Short of Playing Both Sides." The Motley Fool. www.fool.com/investing/mutual-funds/2007/01/11/the-long-and-short-of-playing-both-sides.aspx

Carrel, Lawrence. "ETF-Only 401(k) Plans." *Smart Money*. www.smartmoney.com/etffocus/index.cfm?story=20060531

Carrel, Lawrence. "More Currency ETFs to Debut." *Smart Money*. www.smartmoney.com/etffocus/index.cfm?story=20060621

CFTech. "Dow Jones Averages Chronology 1884–1995." www.cftech.com/BrainBank/finance/dowjonesavgshist.html

ChartwellETFAdvisor.com. www.chartwelletfadvisor.com/

Citi. "Citi Depositary Receipt Services." http://wwss.citissb.com/adr/www/index.htm

CNNMoney.com. "10 Tips to Protecting Your Nest Egg." http://money.cnn.com/2009/01/13/pf/Ask_the_mole.moneymag/index.htm

CNNMoney.com. "Top Sector ETFs." http://money.cnn.com/data/funds/etf/topsectors/

CNNMoney.com. "Various." www.cnnmoney.com

CommodityOnline. "Buy and Hold Strategy Officially Obsolete." www.commodityonline.com/news/Buy-and-hold-strategy-officially-obsolete-14165-3-1.html

Consumer Reports. "Investing: A Bargain Alternative to Mutuals." www.consumerreports.org/cro/money/personal-investing/exchange traded-funds-9-07/overview/0709_investing_ov_1.htm?resultPageIndex=1&resultIndex=1&searchTerm=etfs

Culloton, Dan. "Sector ETFs: Use at Your Own Risk." Morningstar.
http://news.morningstar.com/articlenet/article.aspx?id=166206&_qsbpa=y

Culloton, Dan. "A Surprise Entry in the Race for Actively Managed ETFs."
Morningstar. http://news.morningstar.com/articlenet/article.aspx?id=193350
&_QSBPA=Y&etfsection=Comm4&t1=1187276492

Custodio, Tony. "How Large Are Large-Cap Stocks?" 401Kafe.
www.infoplease.com/finance/tips/money/moneyman_101199.html

Dawson, Chester. "Emerging Markets: Beyond the Big Four."
BusinessWeek. www.businessweek.com/magazine/content/
05_52/b3965450.htm

Delfeld, Carl. "Are HealthShares ETFs Too Specialized?" Chartwell
Advisor at Seeking Alpha. http://seekingalpha.com/article/35024-are-
healthshares-etfs-too-specialized

Dogs of the Dow. "Dow History." www.dogsofthedow.com/dowhist.htm

Dolan, Ronald E., and Robert L. Worden, editors. *Japan: A Country Study*.
(Washington, D.C.: GPO for the Library of Congress, 1994).
http://countrystudies.us/japan/100.htm

Dow Jones Indexes. "Corporate Bond Index."
www.djindexes.com/mdsidx/?event=showCorpBond

The Economist. "Currency Comeback." www.economist.com/displayStory.
cfm?story_id=12494697&source=features_box_main

Elfenbein, Eddy. "Accessing Micro-Caps Via ETFs." Seeking Alpha.
http://seekingalpha.com/article/4440-accessing-micro-caps-via-etfs-etfs-iwc-
fdm-pzi

Ellentuck, Albert B. "Investing in Tax Efficient Funds." All Business. www.allbusiness.com/personal-finance/investing/255356-1.html

Energy Bulletin. www.energybulletin.net/node/37168

ETF Guide. "History of Exchange Traded Funds." www.etfguide.com/exchangetradedfunds.htm

ETF Trends. "Actively Managed" category. www.etftrends.com/actively_managed_/index.html

ETF Trends. "Healthcare" category. www.etftrends.com/healthcare/index.html

ETF Trends. "Retirement" category. www.etftrends.com/retirement/index.html

ETF Zone. "ETF Liquidity Myth Dispelled." http://finance.yahoo.com/etf/education/05

Experiments in Finance. "Diversifying into Real Estate Through REIT ETFs." www.experiglot.com/2006/10/26/diversifying-into-real-estate-through-reit-etfs

Federal Reserve Bank of Atlanta for Jim Cramer quote. http://macroblog.typepad.com/macroblog/2008/10/the-end-of-buy.html

Federal Reserve Bank of Chicago. "Strong Dollar, Weak Dollar." www.chicagofed.org/consumer_information/strong_dollar_weak_dollar.cfm

Federal Reserve Bank of San Francisco. "Ask Dr. Economy." www.frbsf.org/education/activities/drecon/answerxml.cfm?selectedurl=/2001/0102.html

Feldman, Jeffery L. "Interactive Q&A: Jeffrey L. Feldman." http://seekingalpha.com/article/31559-interactive-q-a-jeffrey-l-feldman-creator-of-healthshares-and-founder-and-chairman-of-xshares-group-llc

Fierce Finance. "The Future of ETFs." www.fiercefinance.com/story/the-future-of-etfs/2007-04-10

FinancialPlanning.com. "Investor Psychology Leads to Bad Decisions." www.financial-planning.com/asset/article/630441/investor-psychology-leads-bad-decisions.html

The Financial Times. "Insight: The Flight of the Long Run." www.ft.com/cms/s/0/267900e0-0360-11de-b405-000077b07658.html?nclick_check=1

Fruend Investing. "Value vs. Growth Investing, and the Winner Is ...." http://freundinvesting.com/2008/06/25/value-vs-growth-investing-and-the-winner-is/

Fund Spy. "The Best ETFs for Your IRA." MSN Money. http://moneycentral.msn.com/content/invest/mstar/P147804.asp

Funds 400 Investing Classroom. "Mid-Cap Stocks: What They Are." http://news.morningstar.com/classroom2/course.asp?docId=2996&page=2&CN=com&t1=1192487808

Ghosh, Palash R. "ETFs' Goal: 401(k) Plans." *BusinessWeek.* www.businessweek.com/investor/content/may2005/pi20050519_2637_pi024.htm

Goldberg, Steven. "The Low-Risk Way to Buy Asia." Kiplinger.com. www.kiplinger.com/columns/value/archive/2008/va1209.htm

Grandfather Foreign Exchange Report. http://mwhodges.home.att.net/exchange_rate.htm

Greenwald, Igor. "In Battle of Growth vs. Value, Value Wins." *Smart Money.* www.smartmoney.com/invisiblehand/index.cfm?story=20070717

Hamilton, Adam. "Gold ETF Impact." ZEAL Speculation and Investment. www.zealllc.com/2006/gldetf.htm

Hansard, Sara. "401(k)s Not Enough for Young Workers." www.investmentnews.com/apps/pbcs.dll/article?AID=/20071211/REG/71211006 (based on a GAO report found at http://edlabor.house.gov/publications/401k-GAO-Report-Low-Savings.pdf)

ING. Investing Globally—A World of Opportunity." www.ingfunds.com/v2/investor/common/pages/misc/default.aspx?i=2907

The Independent. "The Gold Boom." www.independent.co.uk/news/business/analysis-and-features/the-gold-boom-403457.html

The Investment Scientist. "Recession and Stock Market Performance." http://investmentscientist.com/2008/01/25/recession-and-stock-market-performance/

Investment U. "Irrational Exuberance." www.investmentu.com/IUEL/2006/20061212.html

Investopedia. "Bond Basics: Different Types of Bonds." www.investopedia.com/university/bonds/bonds4.asp

Investopedia. "Bond ETFs: A Viable Alternative." www.investopedia.com/articles/bonds/05/011105.asp

Investopedia. "Brazil, Russia, India, and China—BRIC." www.investopedia.com/terms/b/bric.asp

Investopedia. "Computing the PEG Ratio and Determining a Company's Earnings Growth." www.investopedia.com/ask/answers/06/pegratioearningsgrowthrate.asp

Investopedia. "Definition of Commodity." www.investopedia.com/terms/c/commodity.asp

Investopedia. "Definition of Small Cap." www.investopedia.com/terms/s/small-cap.asp

Investopedia. "Exchange Traded Notes—An Alternative to ETFs." www.investopedia.com/articles/06/ETNvsETF.asp

Investopedia. "Introduction to Small Caps." www.investopedia.com/articles/01/080101.asp

Investopedia. "Junk Bonds: Everything You Need to Know." www.investopedia.com/articles/02/052202.asp

Investopedia. "Margin Trading: What Is Buying on Margin?" www.investopedia.com/university/margin/margin1.asp

Investopedia. "When Fear and Greed Take Over." www.investopedia.com/articles/01/030701.asp

Investopedia. "Yield." www.investopedia.com/terms/y/yield.asp

Investorwords. "Definition of Collective Trust." www.investorwords.com/5462/collective_trust.html

Jackson, David. "Are Bond ETFs a Good Deal?" Seeking Alpha. http://seekingalpha.com/article/655-are-bond-etfs-a-good-deal

Krantz, Matt. "Now Is a Good Time to Buy Bonds, but Make Sure You Understand Them." USA Today. www.usatoday.com/money/perfi/columnist/krantz/2006-06-06-bonds_x.htm

Kamlet, Art, and George Regnery. "Stocks—American Depositary Receipts ADRs." The Investment FAQ. http://invest-faq.com/articles/stock-adrs.html

Kathman, David. "Five Tips for Smart Sector Investing." Morningstar. http://news.morningstar.com/articlenet/article.aspx?id=185615

Kavussanos, Manolis G., and Stelios Marcoulis. "Risk and Return in Transportation and Other U.S. and Global Industries." Published by Springer, 2001. www.stock-market-crash.net/nasdaq.htm

Lancellotta, Amy B. R. "Actively Managed Exchange Traded Funds."
Investment Company Institute. www.ici.org/statements/cmltr/
02_sec_etfs_com.html#TopOfPage

Larson, Paul. "What Every Would-Be Investor Should Know About China."
Morningstar. http://news.morningstar.com/forbidden/smartarticleslogin2.
html?vurl=http%3a%2f%2fnews.morningstar.com%2farticlenet%2farticle.
aspx%3fid%3d195899&referid=A1598

Lim, Paul. "Money Matters: Is the Emerging Markets Craze Over?" *U.S.
News and World Report*. www.usnews.com/usnews/biztech/articles/070220/
20moneymatters.htm

Little, Ken. "Understanding Price to Earnings Ratio." About.com.
http://stocks.about.com/od/evaluatingstocks/a/pe.htm

Lydon, Tom. "Currency ETFs As an Asset Class." ETF Trends.
www.etftrends.com/2006/09/currency_etfs_a.html

Lydon, Tom. "An ETF Trend-Following Plan for All Seasons." ETF Trends.
www.etftrends.com/2008/07/an-etf-trend-following-plan-for-all-seasons.html

Lydon, Tom. "New Commodities ETF—Investing in Futures."
ETF Trends. www.etftrends.com/2006/02/new_commodities.html

Lydon, Tom. "The Past and Future of ETFs." ETF Trends.
www.etftrends.com/2007/08/as-etfs-prolife.html

Lydon, Tom. "What Constitutes an Emerging Market?" ETF Trends.
www.etftrends.com/emerging_markets/index.html

Maiello, Michael, and Megan Johnson. "2006 Mutual Fund Survey."
Forbes.com. www.forbes.com/free_forbes/2006/0918/142_2.html

Mandel, Michael J., and Margaret Popper. "The Painful Truth About
Profits." *BusinessWeek*. www.businessweek.com/magazine/content/02_44/
b3806001.htm

McCall, Matthew. "Hedge against Corrections with Short ETFs." Investopedia. http://research.investopedia.com/news/IA/2007/Hedge_Against_Corrections_With_Short_ETFs.aspx

McClatchy, Will. "Specialty Medical ETFs." ETFZone at Forbes.com. www.forbes.com/etfs/2007/04/05/xshares-healthshares-medical-pf-etf-in_wm_0404soapbox_inl.html

Middleton, Timothy. "Buy the S&P 500 with Better Returns." *MSN Money*. http://moneycentral.msn.com/content/p100259.asp

Morningstar. "International Investing Center." www.morningstar.com/centers/global.html?t1=1184862607&t1=1184944068

Morris, Sonya. "Avoid These ETFs." Morningstar. http://news.morningstar.com/articlenet/article.aspx?id=174240&_qsbpa=y

The Motley Fool. "Motley Fool Index Center." www.fool.com/school/indexes/sp500.htm

Mueller, Jim. "Growth vs. Value: Real Distinction or Not?" The Motley Fool. www.fool.com/investing/small-cap/2006/04/06/growth-vs-value-real-distinction-or-not.aspx?terms=growth+vs.+value&vstest=search_042607_linkdefault

MSN Money. "State Street Launches First International Treasury Bond ETF." http://news.moneycentral.msn.com/provider/providerarticle.aspx?feed=BW&date=20071005&id=7587309

National Mining Association. "Investing in Gold: Introduction and General Overview of Markets." www.nma.org/statistics/gold/gold_investing.asp

Nusbaum, Roger. "The Future of ETFs." Random Roger. http://seekingalpha.com/article/628-the-future-of-etfs

Nusbaum, Roger. "Ride the Commodities Bull with ETFs." TheStreet.com. www.thestreet.com/etf/etf/10263400.html

Nyaradi, John. "How to Profit Using Sector Rotation." Ezine article.
http://ezinearticles.com/?How-to-Profit-Using-Sector-Rotation&id=791394

Options Outlet. www.optionsoutlet.com/stock_ebooks/technical_analysis_
fromAtoZ/reference_chapter/indicators/moving_averages.html

Oxford Futures. "A Brief History of Commodities." www.oxfordfutures.
com/futures-education/futures-fundamentals/brief-history.htm

Pacific Investment Management Company (PIMCO). "Bond Basics—
Everything You Need to Know."

Pacific Investment Management Company (PIMCO). "Yield Curve Basics."

Pasternak, Carla. "Why Are Income ETFs Taking Off?" Street Authority.
www.streetauthority.com/cmnts/cp/2004/04-05.asp

People's Daily Online. "Beijing's Goal: 18 Million People by 2020."
http://english.peopledaily.com.cn/200411/09/eng20041109_163279.html

Percent of World Market Cap by Country. http://bespokeinvest.typepad.
com/bespoke/2008/06/percent-of-worl.html

Portfolio Solutions. "The Mutual Fund Follies." www.portfoliosolutions.
com/v2/pdf/Chapter10.pdf

Radical Guides. "The Radical Guide to Bonds." www.radicalguides.com/
2005/06/the_radical_gui_1.html

RB Trading. www.rb-trading.com

Reeves, Scott. "ETFs for Retirement." *Forbes*. www.forbes.com/retirement/
2005/06/22/etf-retirement-investing-cx_sr_0622etf.html

Richards, Meg. "Sector ETFs Allow Investing in Trends." *Washington Post*.
www.washingtonpost.com/wp-dyn/articles/A20447-2005Apr2.html

Rocco, William Samuel. "Five Steps to Better International Investing." Morningstar. http://news.morningstar.com/articlenet/article.aspx?id= 189479&_qsbpa=y&globalcsection=moreinfo5&t1=1192555065

Rosevear, John. "Global Investing Made Simple." The Motley Fool. www.fool.com/investing/international/2007/07/19/global-investing-made-simple.aspx

Russell, Michael. "How Are Currency Values Determined?" Ezine article. http://ezinearticles.com/?How-are-Currency-Values-Determined?&id=467643

Scherzer, Lisa. "An Evolution in ETFs." *Smart Money*. www.smartmoney.com/theproshop/index.cfm?Story=20060216

Schoen, John W. "Should I Invest in Commodities?" MSNBC. www.msnbc.msn.com/id/15768192/

Schwartz, Nelson D. "Why Gas Prices Dropped." CNNMoney.com. http://money.cnn.com/magazines/fortune/fortune_archive/2006/10/30/8391681/index.htm

Scientific American. "My Genes Make Me Invest: DNA Implicated in Financial Risk-Taking." www.sciam.com/blog/60-second-science/post.cfm?id=my-genes-made-me-invest-dna-implica-2009-02-10

Securities and Exchange Commission. "Microcap Stock: A Guide for Investors." www.sec.gov/investor/pubs/microcapstock.htm

Securities Industry and Financial Markets Association. "Investing in Bonds." www.investinginbonds.om/learnmore.asp?catid=7&subcatid=86

Seeking Alpha. "Commodity ETFs and ETNs." http://seekingalpha.com/article/30369-commodity-etfs-and-etns

Seeking Alpha. "Investor Psychology and Market Expectations." http://seekingalpha.com/article/108776-investor-psychology-and-market-expectations

Seeking Alpha. "Touchdown! When Do Financial Stocks Hit Zero?" http://seekingalpha.com/article/116732-touchdown-when-do-financial-stocks-hit-zero?source=yahoo

Siegel, Aaron. "Investors Think Globally, Invest Locally." *Investment News*. www.investmentnews.com/apps/pbcs.dll/article?AID=/20070717/REG/7071 7019/-1/INDaily01

Simpkins, Jason. "Why Crude Oil Will Present Investors with a Golden Opportunity in 2009." Money Morning. www.moneymorning.com/2008/12/ 29/oil-2009/

Sjuggerud, Dr. Steve. "Emerging Market Stocks." Investment U. www.investmentu.com/IUEL/2005/20050215.html

Skala, Martin. "ETFs: Low-Cost Way to Invest Abroad." *Christian Science Monitor*. www.csmonitor.com/2005/1006/p16s01-wmgn.html

Smart Money. "Are ETFs Right for You?" www.smartmoney.com/etf/education/index.cfm?story=right2004

Smart Money. "How to Make Money in a Sideways Market." www.smartmoney.com/investing/stocks/how-to-make-money-in-a-sideways-market/

Spence, John. "Barclays' Currency ETNs Dealt a Blow on Taxes." MarketWatch. www.marketwatch.com/news/story/story.aspx?guid= %7B1C874197%2D7CAA%2D463B%2DA700%2DA3B15DD1263F%7D &siteid=rss

Spence, John. "ETNs Face Taxing Times: Lineup of ETF-Like Products Grows, but Tax Advantages in Question." MarketWatch. www.marketwatch. com/news/story/tax-advantages-etn-investments-question/story.aspx?guid=% 7BB54182F3-3946-4CC0-A7A5-73DAE68D45CB%7D

Spence, John. "New ETFs Target Retirement Market." MarketWatch. www.marketwatch.com/news/story/story.aspx?guid=%7B529D466D-F123- 483A-B943-C0EECE97A966%7D&siteid=rss

Spence, John. "Tempest in an Index Fund: Robert Arnott and John Bogle Clash over Best Indexing Strategy." *MarketWatch*. www.marketwatch.com/news/story/rivals-arnott-bogle-spar-over/story.aspx?guid=%7BDAFCCB14-21EA-44E0-B919-A2D484544413%7D

Spence, John. "Trouble in ETF Paradise?" MarketWatch. www.marketwatch.com/news/story/buyer-beware-etf-strategies-become/story.aspx?guid=%7B5C10BD7B%2D4E22%2D4C1F%2D873A%2D680811FF2298%7D

Standard & Poor's. "S&P 500 Description." www2.standardandpoors.com

Stein, Ben. "Anticipating All the Retirement Variables." Yahoo! Finance. http://finance.yahoo.com/expert/article/yourlife/43552

Steinhilber, J. D. "ETFs: Broadening or Perverting Index Investing?" Agile Investing. http://seekingalpha.com/article/27408-etfs-broadening-or-perverting-index-investing

StockCharts.com. "Moving Averages." http://stockcharts.com/school/doku.php?id=chart_school:technical_indicators:moving_averages

Stockhouse. "Profit from Oil's Long-Term Gusher." www.stockhouse.com/Columnists/2008/April/23/Profit-from-oil-s-long-term-gusher

StockMarketingTiming.com. "Nikkei 225, Dow Jones Crash of 1929, and the Popular ETFs." www.stockmarkettiming.com/nikkei-comparison.html

Street Authority. "200-Day Moving Average." www.streetauthority.com/terms/num/200dma.asp

Street Authority. "Simple vs. Exponential Moving Averages." www.streetauthority.com/terms/simpleandexponentialmovingaverages.asp

Taulli, Tom. "Playing Commodities with ETFs." The Motley Fool. www.fool.com/news/mft/2005/mft05042908.htm

TDAX Funds. "TDAX Funds FAQ." www.tdaxshares.com/content/view/39/116/#faq6

TDAX Funds. "TDAX Independence 2040 Overview." www.tdaxshares.com/component/option,com_xshares/Itemid,175/task,viewetf/etfid,16/

Tiburon Strategic Advisors. Tiburon Conference PowerPoint Presentation on Retirement.

Tseng, K. C. "Overconfidence and High-Tech Stocks in the 1990s." Craig School of Business, California State University.

Trading Markets.com. "Watch the 200-Day Moving Average: Here's Why." www.tradingmarkets.com/.site/Swingtrading/Commentary/todaysetfo/-51950.cfm

Trading Markets.com. "What Historical Market Patterns Can Teach Us About the Present." www.tradingmarkets.com/.site/stocks/education/WeeklyCharts/10262001-20547.cfm

Vanguard. "Vanguard 500 Index Fund Investor Shares." https://personal.vanguard.com

Van Schyndel, Zoe. "The ABCs of Currency ETFs." The Motley Fool. www.fool.com/investing/etf/2006/08/15/the-abcs-of-currency-etfs.aspx

Van Schyndel, Zoe. "Fixed-Income Fever." The Motley Fool. www.fool.com/investing/etf/2007/04/04/fixed-income-fever.aspx

Vardy, Nicholas. "Global Investing: Easy As American Pie." Seeking Alpha. http://seekingalpha.com/article/25614-global-investing-easy-as-american-pie

Waldock, Lind. "History of Commodities Exchanges." www.lind-waldock.com/edu/com/com_history.shtml

Wall Street Journal online. "Dollar's Dive Deepens As Oil Soars." http://online.wsj.com/article/SB120423483765800801.html?mod=hpp_us_pageone

Wall Street Journal online. "Political Interference Seen in Bank Bailout Decisions." http://online.wsj.com/article/SB123258284337504295.html

Wall Street Sector Selector. "Buy the Right ETFs at the Right Time." www.wallstreetsectorselector.com/investment_accidents.html

Wherry, Rob. "Are Actively Managed ETFs Worth the Wait?" *Smart Money*. www.smartmoney.com/fundinsight/index.cfm?story=20070719&src=fb&nav=RSS20

Whistler, Mark. "Determining What Market Cap Suits Your Style." Investopedia. www.investopedia.com/articles/mutualfund/06/mfmarketcaps.asp

Wiandt, Jim. "Heavy-Hitting ETFs Could Be the Industry's Ticket." IndexUniverse. www.marketwatch.com/News/Story/Story.aspx?guid=%7BB1D7B090%2D2E02%2D49C8%2DB2DF%2D6C8D5F7982C2%7D&dist=rss&siteid=mktw

Wikipedia. "Commodity Markets." http://en.wikipedia.org/wiki/Commodity_markets

Wikipedia. "Currency." http://en.wikipedia.org/wiki/Currency

Wikipedia. "Emerging Markets." http://en.wikipedia.org/wiki/Emerging_markets

Wikipedia. "Fundamentally Based Indexes." http://en.wikipedia.org/wiki/fundamental_weighting

Wikipedia. "The Global Economy." http://en.wikipedia.org/wiki/the_global_economy

Wikipedia. "Short Finance." http://en.wikipedia.org/wiki/Short_selling

Wikipedia. "South Sea Company." http://en.wikipedia.org/wiki/South_Sea_Bubble

Wikipedia. "Tulip Mania." http://en.wikipedia.org/wiki/Tulip_mania

Wilcox, Cort. "Growth vs. Value: What's the Difference?" CDAPress.com. www.postfallspress.com/articles/2007/07/08/business/bus03.txt

Wood, Carol A. "Real Estate Plays, Hassle-Free." *BusinessWeek*. www.businessweek.com/investor/content/jul2005/pi20050721_3055_pi051.htm

WTRG Economic. "Oil Price History and Analysis." www.wtrg.com/prices.htm

Xinhua. "Beijing's Population Nears 15 Million." www.chinadaily.com.cn/english/doc/2005-04/15/content_434469.htm

Yahoo! Finance. "Vanguard Renews Cost Competition in ETF Market with Introduction of Europe Pacific ETF." Vanguard press release. http://72.14.253.104/search?q=cache:XM9trfMZhscJ:biz.yahoo.com/bw/070725/20070725005136.html%3F.v%3D1+vanguard+etfs+assets&hl=en&ct=clnk&cd=4&gl=us&client=firefox-a

Resources

Books

Appel, Marvin. *Investing with Exchange Traded Funds Made Easy: Higher Returns with Lower Costs—Do It Yourself Strategies Without Paying Fund Managers*. (Upper Saddle River, NJ: FT Press, 2007). This primer focuses on technical ways to buy ETFs.

Bernstein, William. *The Four Pillars of Investing: Lessons for Building a Winning Portfolio*. (New York: McGraw-Hill, 2002). A classic on building a sensible portfolio.

Bogle, John C. *The Little Book of Common Sense Investing: The Only Way to Guarantee Your Fair Share of Stock Market Returns*. (Hoboken, NJ: Wiley, 2007). This condensed version of the wisdom of Jack Bogle is a little gem.

Culloton, Dan, ed. and Morningstar. *Morningstar ETFs 150*. (Hoboken, NJ: Wiley, 2007). Features top ETF funds with the patented Morningstar.

Hebner, Mark. *Index Funds: The 12-Step Program for Active Investors*. (IFA Publishing, 2007). More than you'd ever want to know about indexing, with portfolios dominated by the IFA group.

Lofton, Todd. *Getting Started in Exchange Traded Funds*. (Hoboken, NJ: Wiley, 2007). A reasonably accessible primer on the subject.

Richards, Archie M., Jr. *Understanding Exchange Traded Funds*. (New York: McGraw-Hill, 2007). A useful resource in exploring the subject.

Services

Bloomberg Professional Service. Geared toward active market pros, this single platform tracks all listed and future ETFs through its EXTF function, among thousands of other functions.

Index

FINANCIAL TIMES

In an increasingly competitive world, it is quality
of thinking that gives an edge—an idea that opens new
doors, a technique that solves a problem, or an insight
that simply helps make sense of it all.

We work with leading authors in the various arenas
of business and finance to bring cutting-edge thinking
and best-learning practices to a global market.

It is our goal to create world-class print publications
and electronic products that give readers
knowledge and understanding that can then be
applied, whether studying or at work.

To find out more about our business
products, you can visit us at www.ftpress.com.